Socrates and Alcibiades

Four Texts

Plato: *Alcibiades I*
Plato (?): *Alcibiades II*
Plato: *Symposium* (212c-223b)
Aeschines of Sphettus: *Alcibiades*

The Focus Philosophical Library

Aristotle: De Anima • M. Shiffman
Aristotle: Nicomachean Ethics • J. Sachs
Aristotle: Poetics • J. Sachs
Athenian Funeral Orations • J. Herrman
Descartes: Discourse on Method • R. Kennington
Empire and the Ends of Politics (Plato/Pericles) • S. D. Collins and D. Stauffer
Four Island Utopias (Plato, Euhemeros, Iambolous, Bacon) • D. Clay and A. Purvis
Hegel: The Philosophy of Right • A. White
Liberty, Equality & Modern Constitutionalism, Volume I • G. Anastaplo
Liberty, Equality & Modern Constitutionalism, Volume II • G. Anastaplo
Lucretius: On the Nature of Things • W. Englert
Plato and Xenophon: Apologies • M. Kremer
Plato: Euthydemus • M. Nichols
Plato: Gorgias • J. Arieti and R. Barrus
Plato: Gorgias and Aristotle: Rhetoric • J. Sachs
Plato: Meno • G. Anastaplo and L. Berns
Plato: Parmenides • A. K. Whitaker
Plato: Phaedo • E. Brann, P. Kalkavage, and E. Salem
Plato: Phaedrus • S. Scully
Plato: Republic • J. Sachs
Plato: Sophist • E. Brann, P. Kalkavage, and E. Salem
Plato: Statesman • E. Brann, P. Kalkavage, and E. Salem
Plato: Symposium • A. Sharon
Plato: Theatetus • J. Sachs
Plato: Timaeus • P. Kalkavage
Socrates and Alcibiades: Four Texts • D. Johnson
Socrates and the Sophists • J. Sachs
Spinoza: Theologico-Political Treatise • M. Yaffe

Socrates and Alcibiades

Four Texts

Plato: *Alcibiades I*

Plato (?): *Alcibiades II*

Plato: *Symposium* (212c-223b)

Aeschines of Sphettus: *Alcibiades*

David M. Johnson
Southern Illinois University Carbondale

Focus *an imprint of*
Hackett Publishing Company, Inc.
Indianapolis/Cambridge

Socrates and Alcibiades
Four Texts

Previously published by Focus Publishing/R. Pullins Company

Focus an imprint of
Hackett Publishing Company, Inc.
P.O. Box 44937
Indianapolis, Indiana 46244-0937

www.hackettpublishing.com

ISBN 13: 978-1-58510-069-9

27 26 25 24 5 6 7 8 9

TABLE OF CONTENTS

INTRODUCTION

§1 Enter Alcibiades: Alcibiades in the *Symposium*

Plato's *Symposium* gives an account of a party (Greek *symposium*, literally "drinking together") set at the home of the Athenian tragic poet Agathon two nights after he had won the prize for tragedy at the Lenaea festival of 416 B.C. The guests decided that it ought to be a rather sober party, as some of them were still hung-over from the party on the night of Agathon's triumph. In place of the hard drinking and song that were more usual fare for a symposium, all were to give speeches in honor of Love, the god and the phenomenon (Greek *eros*). Among the guests was Socrates, who had managed to avoid the rowdier event of the night before, but was willing to dress himself up in uncharacteristically fancy garb in order to make an appearance on this night. In the last of the speeches about love, Socrates told what he claimed to have learned about love from Diotima, a wise woman from Mantineia who is otherwise unknown. According to Diotima, the true lover ascends from loving beautiful bodies, to loving beautiful souls, to loving beautiful ideas, and at last to loving one Idea, or Form, Beauty itself. This highest love consists of the vision of "Beauty itself, perfect, pure, undiluted Beauty, not full of human flesh and color and other mortal nonsense, but divine, uniform Beauty itself."[1] In this love for Beauty itself, love for individual human beings is transcended, if not rejected. Passion has become philosophy, albeit rather passionate philosophy. But Plato does not have his *Symposium* end here. Suddenly Alcibiades crashes the party, drunk, colorful and corporeal, full of the very mortal nonsense Diotima had argued should be overcome. And Alcibiades, instead of praising love, praises Socrates, the one unique man he has found, the man he has loved as no other.

On one level Alcibiades' account of Socrates reinforces Diotima's teaching. Alcibiades tells how Socrates rejected his bodily advances, thus

---

[1] *Symposium* 211e. The figure 211e is what is known as a "Stephanus number," taken from Henri Estienne's 1578 edition of the Greek text. Passages in Plato's works are regularly referred to in this way to allow for easy cross-references between different editions and different translations.

showing himself to be above the corporeal nonsense of the lower sorts of love. In some ways Socrates even seems to be a twin for Love—both Love and Socrates are poor hunters in pursuit of beauty and knowledge. But Alcibiades' speech does more than show how Socrates has followed Diotima's teaching. For Alcibiades mixes blame with his praise, and presents a version of love that we may feel more comfortable with than the austere metaphysics of Diotima. In this respect his speech resembles that of Aristophanes (189d–193c), as Plato hints by having Alcibiades barge in just as Aristophanes is about to respond to Socrates. In Aristophanes' speech we are all in search of our other halves, looking for the unique individual who can make us whole. Alcibiades speaks of his love for the one unique man he has found. Are we meant to be tempted by Alcibiades' rival account of love? Does Plato allow us to love individuals, like Socrates—or even Alcibiades? Or is such love but a poor excuse for the abstract vision of Beauty itself?

Alcibiades was also more than just another example of the aristocratic young men fascinated by Socrates: he was the most controversial of Socrates' companions. He was as brilliant as he was prone to scandal, and his inability to remain in favor in his native city (or the Athenians' inability to overlook his flaws in favor of his gifts) contributed mightily to the defeat of Athens by Sparta in 404, just five years before Socrates' trial and execution. It was for the offense of corrupting the youth, together with impiety, that Socrates was put to death. Was Socrates in any way responsible for the ultimate failure of Alcibiades? Socrates tells us he had two loves, philosophy and Alcibiades (*Gorgias* 481d–482b). But what did he see in Alcibiades in the first place? What did he try to teach him, and how did he try to teach it? Why did he fail?

These questions cannot be answered by the *Symposium* alone. But we are lucky enough to have two other Socratic dialogues depicting conversations between Alcibiades and Socrates: the *Alcibiades I* and *Alcibiades II*. Questions about their authenticity have led most scholars to ignore them. But regardless of who wrote them, these two works are philosophically substantial, and hold answers (if not necessarily Plato's answers) to many of the most important questions raised by the relationship between Socrates and Alcibiades. A third work on Socrates and Alcibiades, the *Alcibiades* of the Socratic author Aeschines of Sphettus, has also been neglected, in part because of Aeschines' unjustly low reputation, in part because only fragments of it survive. But the fragments we do have are substantial, and they show that Aeschines' work had much in common with the two Alcibiades dialogues attributed to Plato. Given the debate about authenticity, and the lack of a definite chronology even for the assuredly authentic works of Plato, we cannot now be certain in what order these works were written. Nor can we be sure how accurately they reflect the historical relationship between the two men. But it is clear that these works provide us with a rich discussion of how Athens' greatest philosopher loved and tried to teach her most talented and most ambitious youth—and why Athens turned on both of them.

§2 Alcibiades

> **Dionysus:** The city longs for him, and detests him, and wants to have him.
> . . . .
> **Aeschylus:** It's best not to raise a lion in the city;
> But if it has been raised, cater to its ways.
> *From the discussion of Alcibiades in Aristophanes'* Frogs *of 405 B.C. (lines 1425, 1431–1432)*

Alcibiades was born in 451 B.C., to a family distinguished on both sides (*Alcibiades I* 104a–b).[2] His mother, Deinomache, was a member of the most important family in Athens, the Alcmaeonids, whose members included Pericles, the most powerful man in Athens from around 460 until his death in 429. Alcibiades' father, Cleinias, was also distinguished; he died fighting at the battle of Coroneia in 447, and left Pericles himself as Alcibiades' guardian. Alcibiades entered public life at a very early age; in 427 he was prominent enough to be mentioned twice by the comic poet Aristophanes (in the now lost *Banqueters*), and by 425 he was a member of an important committee revising the tribute quotas for Athens' allies. A few years later, Alcibiades attempted to take advantage of his family's traditional ties with Sparta to gain a major role in the negotiations that led to the Peace of Nicias between Athens and Sparta in 421. He failed at this, but was elected general, the highest political office at Athens, in 420, when he was barely beyond the minimum age of 30 for serving in this position. He was now working to undermine the peace (and his rival Nicias, who had engineered it), and managed to put together a coalition of cities against Sparta. This pressured Sparta into a major battle in 418, but the Athenians only half-heartedly supported Alcibiades' policy, and the Spartans won the battle.

By this time Alcibiades was one of the leading figures in Athens, and almost certainly the most controversial, as well known for his ostentatious display of wealth (compare *Alcibiades I* 104c, 112c–123c) and his scandalous personal life (*Symposium* 216b) as for his diplomacy. In 415, Alcibiades was the main advocate in favor of the fateful expedition against Sicily, and was chosen to lead it, together with his conservative rival Nicias and a third general. A passion for the expedition swept Athens; according to the Platonic *Theages*, Socrates was one of the few to speak out against it (*Theages*

---

[2] Our main sources for Alcibiades' life are his contemporaries Thucydides (5.43 to the end of his history) and Xenophon (*Hellenica*, from the beginning to 2.1) and Plutarch's *Life of Alcibiades*, written nearly 500 years after Alcibiades' death. See also the modern works in the bibliography. Below I cite only passages from the works translated in this volume that may be related to specific events in Alcibiades' life.

129d1). But Alcibiades' extravagant private life and extreme ambition had made him suspect to many Athenians, some of whom even believed that he wished to become tyrant (*Alcibiades II* 141a). As the expedition was about to sail, an act of sacrilege led to a scandal that brought about Alcibiades' fall. The herms, statues of Hermes that stood before many Athenian homes, were defaced one night, and Alcibiades was one of those blamed. Shortly after the fleet's arrival in Sicily, Alcibiades was recalled to face charges on another matter that many connected to the desecration of the herms: a private parody of the Eleusinian mysteries, a very prominent and most secret Athenian rite. Most modern scholars believe that Alcibiades did privately mock the mysteries, but was not involved in the desecration of the herms. But many of the original readers of our texts may have assumed that Alcibiades was guilty on both counts. Alcibiades, at any rate, escaped before he could be brought to trial, and fled to Sparta. The Athenians condemned him to death *in absentia* and confiscated his property. Under the decent but overcautious and superstitious Nicias the Athenian expedition to Sicily would end in disaster for Athens in 413. Perhaps Alcibiades could have led the expedition to success, but without him it would not have been undertaken in the first place.[3]

At Sparta Alcibiades at first enjoyed striking success as an adviser. His advice was instrumental in leading the Spartans to help the Sicilians against Athens and to set up a permanent garrison at Decelea, just outside Athens, which essentially forced the Athenians to remain cramped within the walls of Athens year-round. But Alcibiades also made enemies among the Spartans, most notably King Agis, whose wife Timaea he was widely believed to have seduced (*Alcibiades I* 121b–c). In 412, when he learned that the Spartans intended to have him killed, Alcibiades took refuge with the Persian satrap Tissaphernes, and offered advice to yet another of Athens' traditional enemies. That winter, Alcibiades told the Athenians that he could induce the Persians to switch sides and support Athens, if he were recalled to Athens and the Athenians were to put down the democratic regime that had exiled him. The opponents of democracy at Athens soon realized that Alcibiades did not have this much clout with the Persians, and decided not to send for him. But he was instead recalled by the democratic leaders of the Athenian fleet based on the island of Samos. By this time an oligarchical regime had managed to seize power in Athens, but Alcibiades did Athens a great service by preventing civil war when he restrained the democratic fleet from sailing home to attack the oligarchs.

The oligarchy at Athens soon crumbled, and Alcibiades led the Athenian fleet to a number of victories against the Spartans and their allies. In 407 he

---

[3] A good antidote to Alcibiades' charm is Thucydides' account, at the end of the seventh book of his history, of the slaughter of the last remnants of the grand Athenian expeditionary force as they struggle to drink from the bloody river Asinarus.

was able to return in triumph to Athens. The restored democracy dropped the charges against him, and he led and protected the Athenian procession to Eleusis that had been interrupted by the Spartan garrison at Decelea. By safeguarding the very mysteries he had been charged with parodying, Alcibiades must have hoped to reduce his reputation for impiety. But the war soon took a turn for the worse, as the Spartans began to enjoy more reliable aid from Persia and at last found, in Lysander, a commander who was at least the equal of Alcibiades. Alcibiades confronted the Spartan fleet under Lysander off the coast of Ionia (modern Turkey), but when Lysander declined to fight Alcibiades left, perhaps to help another Athenian fleet or to raise money to pay his rowers. He left his friend and helmsman Antiochus in charge of the fleet at nearby Notium, with orders not to engage the Spartans (see *Alcibiades I* 117d, 125c–d, 135a). But Antiochus fought a battle anyway, and it ended in a defeat, albeit a relatively minor one. Alcibiades attempted to lure Lysander into fighting again, but without success, and his subsequent fund-raising raiding expedition against Cyme, an Athenian ally, raised an outcry.

Alcibiades' enemies latched on to the defeat at Notium, alleging dereliction of duty in leaving the fleet in the command of a helmsman rather than a more senior leader. Charges of personal immorality were probably made as well. Alcibiades was either removed from office, or not reelected. He went into voluntary exile, setting himself up as a sort of robber baron in private holdings just north of the Hellespont (the Dardanelles). In 405 Alcibiades attempted to warn the Athenian admirals of their imprudent strategy at nearby Aegospotami, but the admirals refused his advice and the Athenian fleet was destroyed. With her navy lost, Athens was taken by the Spartans in 404. After the war Alcibiades took refuge with the Persian satrap Pharnabazus, but was soon murdered, probably on the orders of the Spartans and the Thirty Tyrants, the pro-Spartan oligarchy that briefly ruled Athens after the war.

The events of Alcibiades' life are woven into the texture of the works in this volume. Some details in our works appear to allude to the rich anecdotal tradition about Alcibiades, which is most easily accessible in Plutarch's *Life of Alcibiades*—a wonderful text, but one that must be used with caution, as it was written five hundred years after the death of Alcibiades. The more important of these detailed correspondences are footnoted where they occur. Other parallels are more thematic. Alcibiades was a warmonger, as his undermining the Peace of Nicias and advocacy of the Sicilian expedition show; Socrates spends much of the first half of the *Alcibiades I* discussing the roles of justice and advantage in war between cities (*Alcibiades I* 107d–109c, 112a–c, 113d; compare *Alcibiades II* 145b–146a). Alcibiades was a notorious cause of faction at home, and changed sides repeatedly. In the *Alcibiades I*, Socrates and Alcibiades discuss friendship among the citizens (126c–127d), identify Alcibiades' true rivals as foreigners, not his Athenian competitors (119c–120c), and discuss his intellectual waffling (116e–117d). Alcibiades' extravagant personal life was one cause of his falls from grace at Athens and Sparta, and his drunken entrance and shameless speech in the *Symposium* show that side of him, if in a charming manner; in the *Alcibiades I* Socrates tries to teach him about moderation (131b, 133c), albeit in the sense of self-knowledge rather than self-control. Aeschines had Socrates choose Themistocles as a historical parallel for Alcibiades; like Alcibiades, Themistocles led Athens to victories but was eventually rejected by the Athenians, only to find refuge with the Persians (Aeschines fragment 9). Alcibiades (like Socrates) was convicted of impiety; his nocturnal revelries and his talk of statues in the *Symposium* (215b) probably allude to the belief that he was one of those who defaced the herms. In the *Alcibiades I*, Socrates calls on him to look to God (133c); in the *Alcibiades II*, Socrates gives him advice on how to pray. Some of these connections are perhaps less striking than others—discussion of faction at home, for example, may say more about Athenian politics in general than Alcibiades' individual role—but taken together they show that the life of the historical Alcibiades is an essential background for an understanding of our texts. It is no accident that Socrates discusses these themes with this man.

§3 Socrates and Alcibiades

"Socrates does injustice by not recognizing the gods the city recognizes, but introducing new divinities (*daimonia*); he also does injustice by corrupting the youth" (Diogenes Laertius 2.40).[4] So, in all likelihood, went the official charges against Socrates in 399. Xenophon's *Memorabilia* (1.2.12–48) addresses the corruption charge through the examples of Alcibiades and Critias. Critias, Plato's uncle, was an intellectual in his own right, but became the worst of the Thirty Tyrants.[5] Yet neither Xenophon's nor Plato's *Apology* mentions either man by name. At the time of the trial, an amnesty had outlawed prosecution for all crimes committed before the restoration of the democracy in 403. But in other cases this hardly prevented speakers from belaboring past misdeeds as a way of besmirching the defendant (Alcibiades' son, for example, was prosecuted at least twice in the 390s, largely because he was Alcibiades' son: see Isocrates 16 and

[4] Despite what "corruption of the youth" implies to modern ears, and Socrates' professed romantic interest in Alcibiades, it is highly unlikely, given contemporary sexual mores, that Socrates was believed to have corrupted anyone sexually. See the note at *Alcibiades I* 103a.

[5] Critias appears as a character in Plato's *Charmides, Protagoras, Timaeus,* and *Critias,* where he seems to be treated with respect, perhaps because of the family connection. Because he was clearly so vicious, and so hateful to the Athenian democracy, Critias did not inspire the same sort of controversy as Alcibiades, who always had his admirers.

Lysias 14 and 15). Many have argued that Socrates came to grief because he was considered antidemocratic and pro-Spartan: his association with the pro-Spartan Critias and the onetime Spartan adviser Alcibiades would hardly have helped here. But as we do not have the speeches given by Socrates' prosecutors, we cannot be sure whether or not they stressed such political charges.

While the precise importance of Alcibiades to the trial of Socrates remains uncertain, it is certain that he played a large role in the subsequent debate about Socrates. Xenophon, as was noted above, defended Socrates' relationship with Alcibiades and Critias in his *Memorabilia*; he is often thought to have been responding not to the charges made at the trial but to the lost *Accusation of Socrates* written by the sophist Polycrates sometime after 393. Many other Socratic writers also wrote about Alcibiades and Socrates. Phaedo of Elis (the title character of Plato's *Phaedo*) and Euclides of Megara are both credited with an *Alcibiades*, but not a scrap of either survives. Antisthenes, a major figure who would be considered the founder of cynicism, wrote about Alcibiades in at least two works. Our evidence for these works is extremely scrappy, but Antisthenes probably used Alcibiades as a vicious foil for more virtuous characters like Heracles and Cyrus the Great. In Antisthenes' works Alcibiades was charged with incest with his mother and sister, lack of education, and rashness, and praised for his beauty and vigor.

The only major extant treatment of Alcibiades and Socrates not to be included in this volume is that in Xenophon's *Memorabilia* (1.2.12–48). There Xenophon directly meets the charge that Socrates corrupted Critias and Alcibiades. Xenophon argues that both Critias and Alcibiades were already full of political ambition when they came to Socrates, and stayed with him only long enough to learn what they needed to learn in order to surpass their contemporaries. He adds that Socrates did in fact succeed in moderating them for as long as they were with him: they were corrupted by bad company later in their lives. Thus, Xenophon claims, Socrates actually deserves credit for keeping the two men in check for as long as he did. Toward the end of his discussion of Critias and Alcibiades, Xenophon includes a curious conversation in which a young Alcibiades shows up his guardian Pericles by arguing that whenever a city enacts a measure without persuading (all of) the people, even in a democracy, the measure is more an act of violence than true law (*Memorabilia* 1.2.40–46). This, Xenophon says, shows that Alcibiades was always interested in outdoing those active in politics, not in really doing philosophy. But it also reveals that Alcibiades had learned how to argue cleverly from Socrates, and that he was happy to embarrass Athens' leading democrat with such arguments.

Yet Xenophon never shows Alcibiades in conversation with Socrates and, after this initial defense, seems to bend over backwards to avoid reference to Alcibiades elsewhere in his Socratic works. There is no direct reference to the love affair between Alcibiades and Socrates, and no mention of their roles at the battles of Potidaea and Delium, events one would think the general Xenophon would be eager to discuss. There are even passages elsewhere in the *Memorabilia* in which Xenophon seems to have taken elements from conversations in Aeschines and the *Alcibiades I* that were originally credited to Socrates and Alcibiades, but given them to a different interlocutor.[6] On the whole, then, Xenophon attempts to distance Socrates from Alcibiades. The authors of the works in this volume took a different tack.

§4 *Alcibiades I*[7]

The *Alcibiades I* is a philosophical seduction based on the theme of self-knowledge. It appears to be a successful seduction—perhaps Socrates' greatest success. For by the end of the dialogue Alcibiades seems convinced to follow Socrates rather than his own ambitions. Socrates, who regularly wins the argument but fails to win over his interlocutors (take Callicles of the *Gorgias*, who is sometimes made out to be an older version of Alcibiades), here seems to have a convert to philosophy. But we all know how the story ends: Alcibiades fails. Why?

Young Alcibiades is at a crucial point, the transition to adult life that will both make it possible for him to win honor by participating in public life and, as it happens, deprive him of the attention he has received as

---

[6] Compare *Memorabilia* 3.6 with Aeschines' *Alcibiades* (for the mention of Themistocles) and *Alcibiades I* 105b–c and 123d; *Memorabilia* 3.7 with *Alcibiades I* 114b6–115a1; *Memorabilia* 4.1.2 with *Alcibiades I* 131c and *Symposium* 210b–c; and *Memorabilia* 4.2 (especially the first half, and the central speech on self-knowledge) with *Alcibiades I* and Aeschines' *Alcibiades*.

[7] Most contemporary scholars doubt that Plato wrote the *Alcibiades I*, but on insufficient grounds. In antiquity, no one doubted the authenticity of the *Alcibiades I* (though many other works were doubted, including the *Alcibiades II*). The work was widely read, admired, and quoted as Plato's, and some went so far as to make it the first work of Plato on their students' reading lists. The doubts originated, it would seem, with Schleiermacher's condemnation of the dialogue in 1836. Schleiermacher's criticisms, and those of many others, are mainly matters of taste, too often based on superficial readings of the dialogue (all too many have failed to see that Socrates' central speech is highly ironic, for example). The dialogue is attacked for being insufficiently Platonic, too Platonic (i.e., too much like an introduction to Plato), or, somehow, both of these. More technical arguments based on the language of the dialogue have been made, but are no more convincing. The most prevalent argument these days is that it is hard to fit the *Alcibiades I*, which seems to combine early Platonic style with ideas current later in Plato's career, into our conception of Plato's development. But we know too little about Plato's development for such arguments to be conclusive; even the order of the publication of his dialogues, except for a few broad trends, is uncertain. For a reasoned defense of authenticity, see Denyer 2001: 14–26.

an object of romantic interest (131c; see 103a with note). He is confident that his family connections, his wealth, and his good nature will see him through, and is ready to address the Athenian Assembly at once. But Socrates will question whether his material advantages will allow him to meet his immense ambitions. And as for his good nature, it resembles the philosophical nature of Plato's *Republic,* which has the potential for great good or great harm: everything depends on education (*Republic* 6.491a–495b; compare Xenophon, *Memorabilia,* 4.1.2–4, and Plutarch, *Life of Alcibiades* 4.1–3). What the Alcibiades of this dialogue seems most to have going for him is an immense ambition, a passion (*eros*: 124b) for glory. It is largely because his ambitions are so grand that he can be brought to see that his advantages, great as they are, do not suffice. Socrates helps him to see that his ambitions reach well beyond the borders of Athens; this makes him a prime candidate for Socratic philosophical inquiry, which also questions the traditional understanding of things. Paradoxically, then, it may be precisely Alcibiades' passion for glory which makes him a potential philosopher, though this very passion will ultimately destroy him. Socrates therefore does not attempt to stifle this ambition, as we might have expected him to do—or, at least, as we may have expected Xenophon's Socrates, with his emphasis on self-control, to do. Instead Socrates puffs up Alcibiades' ambition, only to show that it is hollow and to attempt to replace it with a philosophical ambition every bit as grand. This is a dangerous strategy, but perhaps the only one likely to have any success with such a man.

If Alcibiades is to win glory and power by advising the Athenians, he had better know what he is talking about. What he will be talking about, Socrates argues, is justice. Alcibiades, though, has never sought out a teacher of justice, or inquired into the matter himself, and thus cannot understand it. But wait: Alcibiades suggests that he has learned it from the many, the people of Athens as a whole. After all, they can teach one some important things, such as how to speak Greek. But people who differ about something clearly cannot understand it; and people differ so much about justice that they kill one another about it—as Alcibiades' own father died fighting for Athens against Sparta. Well, Alcibiades cynically but honestly observes, the Athenians don't really deliberate about justice, but about what is to their advantage. Here Socrates shows Alcibiades that what is admirable (which includes justice) is also good, in large part by making use of Alcibiades' belief that he would admirably choose to risk his life to save a friend rather than advantageously retreat to safety (103a–116e).

By this point, Alcibiades' confidence is beginning to be shaken. His mind wavers; he is confused, because, as Socrates shows him, he thinks he knows what he doesn't know, and this leads to failure. But he has one last rejoinder: he hardly differs from other Athenian political figures in this regard—not even Pericles, whom Socrates quickly shows up. Now Socrates embarks on a colorful and wonderfully ironic speech in apparent praise of the leaders of Athens' great rivals, Sparta and Persia. Their leaders are

Alcibiades' true opponents, but they are better bred, better educated, and better financed than he. If he is to have any chance, he must follow the commandment posted at Apollo's temple at Delphi: know thyself. Here this means that he must recognize who his true rivals are, and how far short he falls of them. If he is to match them, it must be through the only thing poor Greeks have a claim to: wisdom (116e–124b).

This is the surface teaching of the speech, and it is desperately needed by Alcibiades. But there is more to the speech than this. It is striking that Socrates says that the Spartans, who prided themselves on their austerity so much that they outlawed the domestic use of coinage, actually have more cash than the rest of the Greeks put together. They are also praised for the chastity of their queens: but this hardly fits the ancient reputation of Spartan women, beginning with Helen. And, as we have seen, Alcibiades himself was thought to have seduced a Spartan queen. Socrates spends far more time on the corrupt wealth of the Spartans than on their famous virtues. He does say more in praise of the education of Persian kings; contrast the negative account of that education at *Laws* 3.694c–696a, where Plato has the Athenian Stranger attack it as soft and effeminate. But even here Socrates stresses Persian decadence, and the spokesperson of the Persians is not their king but the cruel and overbearing queen mother, Amestris. Thus the point is not only that a mere Athenian cannot compete for world domination with Spartan or Persian kings when it comes to material resources, but to call into question, through cutting irony, whether things such as wealth and ancestry have any value in themselves. Riches corrupt the Spartans and luxury makes the Persians effete. Ancestry is more myth than fact, as Socrates shows by constructing a fanciful divine ancestry for himself to mock Alcibiades' dubious claim to a divine ancestor.

Following this speech, Alcibiades is convinced that he must improve himself (124b). But how? He wants to lead the city, and after questioning comes up with a promising description of how to do so—if one also entirely at odds with his subsequent political career. He, a master of political intrigue, would produce friendship (*philia*) among the citizens. This suggestion seems reasonable and Platonic enough, but Socrates rejects it by claiming that friendship, which he identifies with agreement, is incompatible with doing one's own work, which he identifies with justice. People do not agree about each other's work because they do not know about each other's work: men do not know how to weave and women do not know how to fight (124b–127d).

We come now to the climax of the dialogue. Instead of looking outward, to see what effect an educated Alcibiades would have on the city's foreign or domestic policy, we turn inward. Just who, or rather what, is Alcibiades—or any of us, for that matter? What is this "self" we aim to know and improve? We are not our possessions, our things, for we use them; nor even are we our bodies, for our souls use our bodies. Nor are we soul in its entirety, but the best part of soul, the part that thinks.

There is probably only one analogy that fits. If an eye wanted to see itself, it would need to look to something like a mirror. It could in fact look to the best part, the working part, of another eye, the pupil, and there see itself. So too the soul, if it is to know itself, must look to something like a mirror; it could look to the best part, the working part, of another soul, the intellectual part, which is divine, and there see divine thought. Suspect lines (see the note at 133c) make the full comparison a bit clearer: as a mirror is a better reflector than a pupil, so too is God a better reflector than even the best part of the soul (127d–133c).

The passage is simple in outline but mysterious in its depths, no doubt intentionally so. Socrates does not explicate the comparison, but immediately moves on to apply it, in a rather sketchy way, to the sorts of political issues he and Alcibiades had begun with. Socrates closes by noting that Alcibiades' condition is slavish, and Alcibiades' resolve to care for justice and follow Socrates—instead of being followed by Socrates, as would befit the normal beloved being followed by his older lover—is cast into shadow by Socrates' closing worry that both he and Alcibiades will be overcome by the power of the city (133d–135e).

I can pause here only to note two striking elements in the comparison that is at the heart of the *Alcibiades I*. First, the sort of self-knowledge at issue here is far removed from that we are most accustomed to, the search for a subjective, personal self that is more a matter for psychoanalysis than philosophy. We are all to look for the same thing, not who we are as individuals, but what we are as rational persons.[8] Instead of finding our inner selves we find what is most objectively real, that is, the divine. In the *Symposium*, Alcibiades says he has caught a glimpse of the divine within Socrates, like the little images of the gods within the statues of satyrs (216e–217a, 222a). If we are to make use of the argument of the *Alcibiades I* to understand Alcibiades' failure, that failure consists in his inability to see that what is divine is shared, at least inasmuch as we all share the sort of rationality that Socrates embodies. For Alcibiades mistakenly believes that Socrates, unlike any other man, is unique (221c–d). This is why he so readily forgets Socrates' arguments once he leaves Socrates' presence (216b).

Finally, the act of looking into another's eyes is full of erotic potential (consider *Phaedrus* 255c–e, *Cratylus* 420a–b). But, despite the fact that Socrates claims at the beginning and the end of this dialogue to be Alcibiades' lover, this erotic element is utterly absent here. The *Alcibiades I* is therefore ever so much duller than the *Symposium* in this regard. But wouldn't Diotima have been proud of Socrates for leaving anything bodily so far behind?

---

[8] See Annas 1985: 121–122; Johnson 1999.

§5 *Alcibiades II*[9]

Alcibiades is on his way to pray to a god—which god we are never told—but seems preoccupied. Socrates soon gives him plenty of reasons to hesitate before praying. For many have thought they were praying for good things, but have in fact been praying for evils. Take Oedipus, who prayed that his sons kill one another. But, Alcibiades replies, he was mad: no one in his right mind would pray for such things. This takes us to a discussion of the different types of madness. Socrates and Alcibiades initially assume that there is only one sort of madness, and that all who are not sensible (or wise) are mad; but this would populate the city largely with wild madmen and make it unlivable, which it is not. Most people, though, including Alcibiades, are foolish enough to pray for and accept tyranny, or the office of general, or children. But all of these more often harm than help: tyrants are murdered, elected generals are prosecuted by their political enemies, and children, even those who turn out well, too often die and leave their parents worse off than if they had never been born. Best then, to pray simply for good things, as a certain poet once said. Alcibiades agrees: our ignorance does lead us astray (135a–143c).

But rather as he had dissected madness, Socrates now dissects ignorance. For if, heaven forbid, Alcibiades wanted to kill his mother or his guardian, Pericles, but didn't know where they were, this ignorance would do him good. The knowledge one really needs is knowledge of what is best. All other sorts of knowledge, whether it be how to wage war, or how to persuade the Assembly, are worse than useless without this knowledge. Homer implies as much, enigmatically, when he says that Margites knows many things, but knows them all badly, for he does not know what is best. This shows that the poet who told us simply to pray for good things was right. And indeed the Spartans follow his advice, or have figured out as much themselves. For while the Athenians offer far more lavish sacrifices, the reverent Laconic prayer for what is good and admirable finds more favor with the gods than do all the expensive Athenian offerings. The gods cannot be bribed (143c–150b).

---

[9] Few scholars today are willing to defend the authenticity of the *Alcibiades II*, save for those (such as Pangle in his introduction to Pangle 1987) who would accept the entire Thrasyllan corpus of Plato, that is, all of the dialogues Thrasyllus gathered into tetralogies during the first century A.D. and considered authentic. It has been argued that the argument about madness (138c–140e) is aimed against the Stoic, or Cynic, position that all who are not wise are mad, and would have been most at home in the skeptical Academy of Arcesilaus (from 268 to 242 B.C.). But Xenophon (*Memorabilia* 1.2.49–50, 3.9.6–7) has Socrates discuss madness in similar terms. There are again linguistic arguments, perhaps stronger than those against the *Alcibiades I*. The dialogue clearly alludes to passages from the *Alcibiades I* (see the notes at *Alcibiades II* 141b, 145b, and 148a for some examples), but this calls out for interpretation before serving as a ground for condemnation.

What is Alcibiades to do, then? Not to pray at all, for if he prays for something specific, he may mistakenly pray for something harmful, and he is insufficiently humble to stick to the simple Spartan prayer for what is admirable and good. No, he must wait for someone to remove the mist from his eyes, the mist that prevents him from seeing what is good and what is evil. That person is to be Socrates, and so it is to Socrates, rather than the god, that Alcibiades gives his wreath. This Socrates regards as every bit as good an omen as that once seen by Creon, when he saw Teiresias approaching wearing such a wreath (150b–151c).

The teaching of the dialogue seems Socratic enough. Socrates says elsewhere that the gods are not impressed with the expense of our sacrifices, and that we should pray simply for what is good.[10] The idea that the only knowledge that counts is knowledge of what is best is also Socratic; it culminates, of course, in the Platonic idea that the greatest form of knowledge is knowledge of the good. Even the discussion of madness, which has seemed post-Socratic to some, has some parallels in Xenophon (*Memorabilia* 1.2.49–50, 3.9.6–7), though it may still be argued that it would be most at home in a later context.

What makes the dialogue most interesting are its puzzles, which should serve as opportunities for interpretation before they provide grounds for attacking the dialogue's authenticity. One is its extraordinarily rich store of allusions to poetry and myth. This first of these allusions is to Oedipus (138c), who seems to have a thematic significance for the dialogue as a whole. Oedipus cursed his sons in a rage, but was hardly the sort of madman who was regularly a threat to public safety. Alcibiades also is foolish but not insane. When warning Alcibiades of the dangers of ambition, Socrates, strangely, adds having children to the standard example of seizing tyranny and the analogous, if legitimate, ambition to be elected to the generalship, the highest and therefore most precarious office at Athens (141d–142c). If any child brought his parents grief, it was Oedipus, and Oedipus is introduced as a father who cursed his sons. Oedipus was also a ruler, technically a tyrant, and while he gained power not through a coup but through his heroic victory over the Sphinx, rule brought him incest with his mother and cursed his city. Oedipus, of course, did not know who his father and his mother were. Socrates, most oddly, suggests scenarios in which Alcibiades would be lucky not to know who his mother or his guardian Pericles were. He would have Alcibiades imagine that he wanted to kill his mother and Pericles (143c–144c). Now of course Alcibiades wished none of this, but it is likely enough that he did feel a

[10] On prayer, Xenophon has Socrates say that one should simply pray for what is good, and make offerings in accord with one's means (*Memorabilia* 1.3.2); compare the argument against doing commerce with the gods in the *Euthyphro* (14e–15a). For the argument that not all knowledge is beneficial, compare *Memorabilia* 4.2.31–32; for the claim that only knowledge of a certain sort is necessary, see, for example, *Euthydemus*, 281d.

kind of rivalry with Pericles, and Antisthenes went so far as to claim that Alcibiades had an incestuous relationship with his mother.[11] What to make of all of this? Readers will have to judge for themselves, but I suggest that the fundamental failing of both Alcibiades and Oedipus may be the absence of self-knowledge.

Another puzzle is the relationship between the *Alcibiades II* and the *Alcibiades I*. The *Alcibiades II* clearly alludes to the *Alcibiades I* on a number of occasions (as at 141b, 145b, and 148a); it also represents a conversation that would have taken place after that of the *Alcibiades I*. Has Alcibiades made any progress? Well, in the *Alcibiades I* Socrates told Alcibiades to look to the divine, and he is now off to pray. But Alcibiades has not thought through what prayer involves, and his praying, which is presumably to be conventional in all save the extraordinary extent of what he will pray for, is hardly the sort of divine quest that Socrates seems to have had in mind. In any event, Socrates convinces Alcibiades not to pray. Instead, he will wait to have Socrates remove his ignorance of good and evil, as Athena removed the mist from Diomedes' eyes, so Diomedes could tell man from god. Alcibiades would seem to need the sort of help Athena gave, for he seems to mistake Socrates for a god, giving him the wreath he had intended for the god. Surely this must seem impious.

Socrates' response, in the last lines of the dialogue, is that this is a good omen, every bit as good as the omen occasioned by the sight of Teiresias to Creon in Euripides' *Phoenician Women*.[12] Socrates therefore hopes that he will be able to defeat Alcibiades' other lovers, as Creon thought that Teiresias' appearance presaged victory for their city, Thebes. But hasn't Socrates already said that Alcibiades was being abandoned by his other lovers (*Alcibiades I* 131d)? All, perhaps, save the people of Athens, whom Socrates still feared at the end of the *Alcibiades I*. Teiresias, for his part, told Creon that Thebes could be saved, but only if his son Menoeceus were sacrificed to save it. Creon refused to sacrifice his son, but his son killed himself to save the city. If we are to read the final poetic allusion in this way, and Socrates is playing the role of Creon, Alcibiades would play Menoeceus, hence Socrates' son, and Athens would be Thebes. Socrates was not willing to sacrifice Alcibiades for Athens, perhaps by withholding from him the teaching that made him an even more powerful politician when he abandoned philosophy for political life. Alcibiades for his part surely did not kill himself for Athens' sake, as Menoeceus had killed himself for Thebes, and Athens, unlike Thebes, was defeated.

---

[11] For the rivalry, consider *Memorabilia* 1.2.40–46 and Plutarch, *Life of Alcibiades* 7.

[12] For the details of the myth, see the note at *Alcibiades II* 151b.

§6 Aeschines' *Alcibiades*

Aeschines, who is often called "Aeschines of Sphettus" (Sphettus being Aeschines' *deme* in Attica) or "Aeschines Socraticus" to distinguish him from the better-known Aeschines, the famous opponent of Demosthenes, was probably a few years younger than Plato. He was a close associate of Socrates: Plato has Socrates name Aeschines as one of the associates he has not corrupted in the *Apology* (33e), and places him at the death scene of the *Phaedo*. Unlike Plato, Aeschines was poor, and had to take pay for teaching; but he did not dare to set up a formal school to rival Plato's. He was credited with seven Socratic dialogues, all now lost. They were admired in antiquity, especially for their style. Moderns have tended to slight his philosophical importance, but it has recently been argued that it was Aeschines who was the first to depict Socrates' view of love.[13] We are even less sure of the dates of his works than we are of those of Plato, but it seems most likely that his *Alcibiades* was composed prior to the other works in this volume; it is nonetheless placed last here because its fragmentary nature makes it the most difficult to appreciate. Alcibiades was a subject in at least one other work of Aeschines, the *Axiochus*, a dialogue named after Alcibiades' paternal uncle. But we know only that Alcibiades was evidently reproached in it for overindulgence in wine, other men's wives, and cockfighting.

In the fragments of the *Alcibiades* Socrates relates a conversation he had with Alcibiades some time ago, and then comments on his relationship to Alcibiades. The original conversation took place early in the relationship between Socrates and Alcibiades, and thus presumably in the years before the outbreak of the Peloponnesian War in 431, about the same time as the conversation of the *Alcibiades I*. Socrates' narration of the dialogue was apparently set at a time when he no longer believed he could help Alcibiades (see fragment 12), and so perhaps fell near the dramatic date of the *Symposium* and thus around the time of Alcibiades' death following the end of the war. As in the *Alcibiades I*, Alcibiades was arrogant and overconfident. But he was soon shown, in part through comparison with Themistocles, that he had much work to do if he was to fulfill his ambitions. Our fragments close with Socrates' remarking that it was through love, not knowledge, that he had believed that he could aid Alcibiades.

The basic structure of the dialogue—save for the narrative form—closely resembles that of the *Alcibiades I*. In particular, note that Socrates' long speech about Themistocles (fragment 9) played much the same role as Socrates' speech about Spartan and Persian kings in the *Alcibiades I*. Aeschines' work takes the natural historical parallel for Alcibiades:

---

[13] So Kahn 1994.

Themistocles, like Alcibiades, was a democrat, a bold and successful military man, and like him ultimately ended his life as an exile in Persian territory. Aeschines probably had Alcibiades claim that just as Themistocles succeeded by means of his natural gifts alone, so too would he. Socrates responds by arguing that Themistocles started out badly—so badly that he was disinherited by his father—and thus clearly wasn't born with the skill he later came to possess (fragment 7). In his long speech in praise of Themistocles, Socrates points out that he was able to defeat the Persian king Xerxes by the sheer power of his intellect, despite Xerxes' superior resources in ships, men, and wealth. Themistocles was so much more clever than the Great King, in fact, that he convinced Xerxes that he had befriended him when he had not, and was later able to retire in grand style to Persia when he was exiled by the Athenians. This speech had a great effect on Alcibiades, who broke out into tears, put his head on Socrates' lap, and, in despair at how short he fell of Themistocles, begged Socrates to help him improve himself (fragment 10).

But Socrates does not simply make Themistocles a positive example: he ended his life in exile, as Alcibiades would. Aeschines may have had Socrates spell out why Themistocles ultimately failed. But the remaining fragments of the dialogue do not provide us with any evidence that he did so. I suspect that any specific failure of policy would be beside the point: we are meant, rather, to see something fundamentally ironic in Themistocles' career. It is not any failure of intellect on his part that leads to his downfall, but his failure to recognize the proper arena in which to use his intellect. He is able to compensate for all the king's riches and all the king's men, but the fickle Athenians first block his plan to cut off Xerxes' escape and then exile him, despite the fact that it was thanks to him alone that they were saved from Xerxes in the first place. He is rich in exile, and has showed himself the most powerful of men, through his intellect; but this ended up meaning nothing, because his goals—power and glory—proved fleeting. At the end of his life he owed what status he retained to the very man he had defeated.

If this is right, Aeschines' argument works on two levels. First, his Socrates is pointing out that Alcibiades, at 20, is no Themistocles, and needs to better himself if he is going to achieve anything comparable. But second, and more fundamentally, Socrates hints that Themistocles' downfall shows the futility of political ambition even in hands as capable as those of Themistocles. The teaching is essentially at one with that of the *Alcibiades I*, where Socrates compares Alcibiades with the kings of Sparta and Persia not only to show how far he falls short of them but also, through irony, to show the emptiness of such worldly ambitions.

Aeschines' work closed with Socrates' remarks on the power of love. It is through love, not through some art, that he thought that he could benefit Alcibiades. The fragments do not make it entirely clear how Socrates expected this to work. One thinks first that Socrates' love for Alcibiades somehow gave him the inspiration to help the young man, or at least to think he could do so. But Aeschines could also be referring to Alcibiades' love for Socrates. As we read in both the *Alcibiades I* (135d) and the *Symposium* (222b), Alcibiades, breaking with the asymmetrical convention of such relationships, came to love Socrates rather than simply being loved by him. Aeschines wrote in his *Aspasia* about the power of love to lead one to improve oneself. He recounted how Aspasia, the famous courtesan who was Pericles' longtime companion, advised none other than Xenophon and his wife that they should aim to make themselves more lovable by making themselves better. When we are in love, we desire to better ourselves for those we love. Hence, perhaps, Alcibiades' shame before Socrates in the *Symposium* (216b). I suggested above that Alcibiades' love for glory was one means that Socrates hoped to use to turn him toward philosophy. Here we see another sort of love at work, though its workings remain mysterious. But it too has its dangers. Alcibiades came to love Socrates, but not to love philosophy. Without this greater love he was overcome by his love for the glory only the fickle people of Athens could give—and take away.

§7 Translator's note

All translation is a compromise, and readers who are wondering whether the *Alcibiades I* or *Alcibiades II* is worthy of Plato should keep in mind that the quality of the writing they read is as much dependent on the compromises—and skill—of the translator as on the quality of the original. Translations of Plato range from the literary to the literal. I aim here to be as literal as I can without reaching the sort of literalism that requires readers to learn a translator's pidgin that lies somewhere between English and Greek. I thus do not aspire to the eloquence of a literary translation, which is on another level truer to the eloquence of Plato (and, it should be said, of much in the non-Platonic or dubiously Platonic works in this volume). This would require a greater sacrifice in consistency (as in the translation of key terms) and a greater interpretive license than I wish to take upon myself. Readers who wish to experience a translation that aims to more fully capture Plato's style should consult Avi Sharon's fluent translation of the *Symposium*, also available from the Focus Philosophical Library.

BIBLIOGRAPHY

Annas, Julia. 1985. "Self-Knowledge in Early Plato." In *Platonic Investigations*, ed. Dominic J. O'Meara, 111–138. Washington, D.C.: Catholic University Press. [On the *Alcibiades I*.]

Brickhouse, Thomas C., and Nicholas D. Smith. 1989. *Socrates on Trial*. Oxford: Oxford University Press.

Carlini, Antonio, ed. and trans. 1964. *Platone: Alcibiade, Alcibiade Secondo, Ipparco, Rivali*. Turin: Boringhieri. [The most up-to-date modern edition of the Greek text, with an Italian translation.]

Davidson, James N. 1997. *Courtesans & Fishcakes: The Consuming Passions of Classical Athens*. New York: St. Martin's.

Denyer, Nicholas, ed. 2001. *Plato: Alcibiades*. Cambridge: Cambridge University Press. [Keyed to the Greek, but with much for the English-only reader.]

Dover, Kenneth, ed. 1980. *Plato: Symposium*. Cambridge: Cambridge University Press. [Also keyed to the Greek, but with much for the English-only reader.]

Ellis, Walter M. 1989. *Alcibiades*. London: Routledge.

Foucault, Michel. 1988. *Technologies of the Self: A Seminar with Michel Foucault*. Ed. Luther H. Martin, Huck Gutman, and Patrick H. Hutton. Amherst: University of Massachusetts Press. [Chapter 2 has much on the *Alcibiades I*.]

Gabriele Giannantoni, ed. 1990. *Socratis et Socraticorum Reliquiae*. 2nd edition. Naples: Bibliopolis. [The standard edition of the fragments of the minor Socratics; Greek text with Italian commentary.]

Gargarin, Michael. 1977. "Socrates' Hybris and Alcibiades' Failure." *Phoenix* 31: 22–37.

Gribble, David. 1999. *Alcibiades and Athens: A Study of Literary Presentation*. Oxford: Clarendon Press.

Hansen, Mogens Herman. 1995. *The Trial of Sokrates—from the Athenian Point of View*. Royal Danish Academy of Sciences and Letters, Historisk-filosofiske Meddelelser 71. Copenhagen.

Howland, Jacob. 1990. "Socrates and Alcibiades: Eros, Piety, and Politics." *Interpretation* 18: 63–90. [On the *Alcibiades II*.]

Johnson, David M. 1999. "God as the True Self: Plato's *Alcibiades I*." *Ancient Philosophy* 19: 1–19.

Kahn, Charles. 1994. "Aeschines on Socratic Eros." In *The Socratic Movement*, edited by Paul A. Vander Waerdt, 87–106. Ithaca: Cornell University Press.

Nussbaum, Martha C. 1986. *The Fragility of Goodness: Luck and Ethics in Greek Tragedy and Philosophy*. Cambridge: Cambridge University Press. [Chapter 6 is on Alcibiades' speech from the *Symposium*.]

Pangle, Thomas, ed. 1987. *The Roots of Political Philosophy: Ten Forgotten Socratic Dialogues*. Ithaca: Cornell University Press. [Includes a translation and interpretation of the *Alcibiades I*.]

Sharon, Avi, trans. 1998. *Plato's Symposium*. Focus Philosophical Library. Newburyport, Mass.: Focus Publishing/R. Pullins Co.

Stone, I. F. 1988. *The Trial of Socrates*. New York: Little, Brown & Co.

ALCIBIADES I

103A **Socrates:** Son of Cleinias, I think you're wondering why I, the first to love you, alone have not stopped loving you when the others have, and why, when the others crowded you with their conversation, I for so many years never said a thing to you.[1] The cause of this was nothing human, but a certain divine opposition:[2] you will be

B told of its power later as well. Now, since it is no longer opposing me, I have approached you like this, and I am of good hope that it will not oppose me in the future.

Now I'm pretty well aware, after watching all this time, of how you've acted toward these lovers. Though they were many and proud,[3] there's not one who has not been surpassed by you

104A in pride and fled. I'd like to go through the reason for your

---

[1] In the asymmetrical form of homosexuality practiced by aristocratic Athenians of his time, Alcibiades' would-be lovers would mainly have been men in their twenties. The younger partner was expected to play hard to get, and to be interested in such relationships not for sexual satisfaction but for some other motive, such as friendship, status, or gaining a mentor among the elite. Alcibiades has just entered his twentieth year (123d) and is, by conventional standards, nearly over the hill for the role of the beloved (131c–d; compare *Protagoras* 309a). Other sources tell us that Alcibiades, while he spurned many, was also quite promiscuous: Socrates is flattering him. On Greek sexuality see Dover 1980: 3–5 and Davidson 1997; for Alcibiades and sexuality see now Gribble 1999: 69–82.

[2] Socrates refers to his divine sign (*daimonion*), which often opposes him and never urges him on. But here as elsewhere Socrates can infer positive guidance from its silence (*Apology* 40a–c; see also *Apology* 31c–d, *Theaetetus* 151a, *Theages* 128d–131a).

[3] Greek *mega phronein* and its cognates (here *megalophrōn*) are here translated by "proud" and its cognates; they can describe qualities ranging from noble high spirits and well-placed confidence to arrogance. For Alcibiades' pride see just below, and contrast 119d.

surpassing pride. You say that you have no need of anyone for anything, for your advantages are so great that you lack nothing, beginning with your body and ending with your soul. First of all, you think that you are most beautiful and tall—and it's clear to all to see that you're not mistaken in this. Next, you think that you are a member of the most active family in your city,[4] which is the B greatest city of Greece, and that you have many excellent friends and relatives there on your father's side, who would serve you should there be any need, and that those on your mother's side are no worse or fewer than these. And greater than all these I've mentioned put together, you think, is the power that you have in Pericles,[5] son of Xanthippus, whom your father left as guardian to you and your brother. He has the power to do what he wants to not only in this city, but in all of Greece, and among many great C nations of barbarians. I'll also add that you are wealthy, but you seem to me to pride yourself least on this. Boasting about all of these things you've defeated your lovers—and it's because of their inferiority that you've defeated them, which has not escaped you. For this reason I know well that you wonder just what I have in mind in not giving up my love and what hope I have in remaining after the others have fled.

Alcibiades: And yet perhaps, Socrates, you don't know that you've D barely beaten me to it. For I intended, you know, to come forward first to ask you this very thing: just what you wanted, and what hope you looked to in crowding me by always taking care to be wherever I was. I really wonder what you're up to, and would be very glad to find out.

Socrates: So it's likely that you'll listen to me eagerly—if, as you say, you desire to know what I have in mind. Am I to speak on the assumption that you'll stay and listen?

Alcibiades: Definitely. Just tell me.

E **Socrates:** Well, look out. For it wouldn't be surprising, you know, if, just as I had trouble starting, I should have trouble stopping.

Alcibiades: Speak on, my good man—I will listen.

---

[4] Alcibiades' mother and his guardian, Pericles, were members of the powerful Alcmaeonid family.

[5] Pericles, the dominant leader in Athens from approximately 460 till his death in 429, became Alcibiades' guardian when Alcibiades' father Cleinias was killed at the battle of Coroneia in 447.

Socrates: So speak it is. It's a hard thing for a lover to approach a man who does not yield to lovers, but nevertheless I must bring myself to point out what I have in mind.

If I, Alcibiades, saw that you were content with what I've mentioned just now, and saw that you thought that you had to 105A live out your life on those terms, I'd have given up my love long ago, or so I persuade myself. But now I will accuse you, face to face, of having other intentions, so that you can recognize that I have kept my mind on you constantly.

It seems to me that if some god said to you, "Alcibiades, do you want to go on living with what you now have, or would you rather die at once if it will not be possible for you to acquire more?" you'd choose, it seems to me, to die. And I'll point out just what hope you're living for. You believe that as soon as you come before the B Athenian people— which you believe will happen within a very few days[6]—coming before them you will show the Athenians that you deserve to be honored as neither Pericles nor anyone else who has lived has been honored, and that after showing this you will have the greatest power in the city, and that if you are the greatest here, you will also be the greatest among the other Greeks, and not only among Greeks but also among the barbarians who inhabit the same continent as we do. And if this same god said to you that you must C reign here in Europe, but that it would not be possible for you to cross into Asia or be active in affairs there, it again seems to me that you would be unwilling to live even under these terms, unless you were going to fill practically all people with your name and your power. And I think you believe that no one other than Cyrus and Xerxes is worth talking about.[7]

Now I know well that you have this hope—I'm not guessing. Perhaps, though, you might say, since you know that what I'm saying is true, D "Well, Socrates, how is this relevant for you?" I'll tell you, dear son of Cleinias and Deinomache: it will be impossible for you to accomplish all the things you have in mind without me. So great is the power that I think I have regarding your affairs and you. And this is why, I think, the god I was waiting for, to allow me to speak with you, did not allow me to speak for so long. For just as you hope

---

[6] Alcibiades has just gained the legal right to address the Athenian Assembly now that he has entered his twentieth year (123d), but the Athenians expected older men to speak first. For an account of his debut, see the note at 120a below.

[7] Cyrus founded the Persian Empire, which he then ruled from 557 to 530. Xerxes, king of the Persians from 486–465, led the Persian invasion of Greece that was defeated in 479.

E to show in the city that you are worth everything to her, and that once you have shown this there will at once be nothing that you won't have the power to do, so too do I have great hope in your case, that I will have the power to show you that I am worth everything to you, and that neither guardian nor relative nor anyone else other than me will suffice to give you the power you desire—with the god's help, of course. So, when you were young and were not yet full of so much hope, the god, it seems to me, did not allow me to talk with you, so 106A that I would not talk in vain. Now he has permitted it, for now you may listen.

Alcibiades: You seem far stranger to me now, Socrates, that you've begun to speak, than when you followed me in silence—though you were quite a strange sight even then. Whether I have these things in mind or not, you've decided, it seems, and even if I deny it, it will get me no closer to persuading you. Well, if I really have had these things in mind, how is it that they will come to pass for me through you and that without you they could not happen? Can you tell me?

B **Socrates:** Are you asking if I can give some long speech of the sort you're accustomed to hearing? That's not my way. But I could show you, I think, that this is the case, if you were willing to do me one small service.

Alcibiades: Well, I'm willing—at least if the service you mention isn't difficult.

Socrates: Does it seem difficult to answer what's asked?

Alcibiades: No.

Socrates: Answer then.

Alcibiades: Ask away.

Socrates: Am I to ask on the assumption that you have the things in mind I say you do?

C **Alcibiades:** So be it, if you want, so I can know what you're going to say.

Socrates: Come on, then, since you have it in mind, as I say, to come forward to advise the Athenians not long from now. If, when you were about to mount the podium, I took hold of you and asked, "Alcibiades, what is it that the Athenians intend to deliberate about that leads you to rise up to advise them? Is it because it's about something you understand better than they do?" What would you answer?

D **Alcibiades:** I'd say, surely, that it's about something I know better than they do.

Socrates: So it's about the things you know that you are a good adviser.

Alcibiades: Why, of course.

Socrates: Now don't you know only those things that you learned from others or discovered by yourself?

Alcibiades: What else could I know?

Socrates: Then is there any way you could have learned or discovered anything if you did not want to learn it or to seek it out it by yourself?

Alcibiades: There's not.

Socrates: And would you want to seek out or learn something that you thought you understood?

Alcibiades: Certainly not.

E **Socrates:** So for whatever you understand now, there was a time when you did not believe that you knew it.

Alcibiades: Necessarily.

Socrates: Well, I myself pretty well know what you've learned. If anything has escaped me, say so. You learned, as far as my memory goes, to read and write, to play the lyre, and to wrestle—but you weren't willing to learn the aulos.[8] These are the things you understand, unless you somehow escaped my notice and learned something else. I think you did not, since neither by night nor by day did you go outside without my noticing it.

Alcibiades: Well, I haven't gone to any teachers other than those.

107A **Socrates:** So is it when the Athenians are deliberating about how to spell that you will rise to advise them?

Alcibiades: Not I, by Zeus.

Socrates: Well, is it when they are deliberating about notes on the lyre?

---

[8] Alcibiades received a traditional Athenian education in grammar, poetry, music, and athletics. Plutarch (*Life of Alcibiades* 2.5) reports that Alcibiades rejected the aulos, a double-reed instrument similar to the oboe, because playing it distorted one's appearance and did not allow one to speak.

Alcibiades: Not at all.

Socrates: Nor, in fact, are they accustomed to deliberating about wrestling moves in the Assembly, either.

Alcibiades: No, they aren't.

Socrates: So it's when they're deliberating about what? For it's not, I suppose, when they're deliberating about building.

Alcibiades: Certainly not.

Socrates: For about this, at any rate, a builder will give better advice than you.

B **Alcibiades:** Yes.

Socrates: Nor is it when they deliberate about divination.[9]

Alcibiades: No.

Socrates: For a diviner would do this better than you.

Alcibiades: Yes.

Socrates: Whether he's short or tall, or beautiful or ugly, or even noble or of low birth.

Alcibiades: Why, of course.

Socrates: For, I think, advice about each thing is a matter for the one who knows, and not for one who's wealthy.

Alcibiades: Why, of course.

Socrates: And whether the one who is making a recommendation is poor or rich will make no difference to the Athenians when they C are deliberating about the health of the people in the city, but they will seek a doctor for their adviser.

Alcibiades: That's likely.

Socrates: So what is it the Athenians will be considering, when you will get up to advise them and be correct to do so?

Alcibiades: Their own affairs, Socrates.

Socrates: Do you mean those of their affairs that have to do with shipbuilding, what sorts of ships they should have built?

Alcibiades: No, I don't, Socrates.

---

[9] Diviners used both divine inspiration and quasi-rational techniques to foretell the future by interpreting dreams, the flight of birds, and the entrails of sacrificial animals. They often advised the Assembly.

Socrates: For you don't, I think, understand how to build a ship. Is this the reason, or is it something else?

Alcibiades: No, that's it.

D **Socrates:** Well, which of their own affairs do you mean?

Alcibiades: When they are deliberating about war, Socrates, or peace, or some other of the affairs of the city.

Socrates: Do you mean when they are deliberating about whom they should make peace with, and whom they should war against, and in what way?

Alcibiades: Yes.

Socrates: And shouldn't they wage war with those it is better to wage war against?

Alcibiades: Yes.

E **Socrates:** And at that time when it is better?

Alcibiades: Of course.

Socrates: And for as long a time as is better?

Alcibiades: Yes.

Socrates: Now if the Athenians were to deliberate about whom they should wrestle with and whom they should spar with, and in what way, would you give better advice, or the trainer?

Alcibiades: The trainer, surely.

Socrates: Can you say what it is the trainer looks to when he advises who one should wrestle with and who not, and when, and in what way? This is the sort of thing I mean: Should one wrestle with those it is better to wrestle with, or not?

Alcibiades: One should.

108A **Socrates:** And as much as is better?

Alcibiades: That much.

Socrates: And also at that time when it is better?

Alcibiades: Of course.

Socrates: Now, one who is singing should sometimes accompany the song with lyre playing and dancing.

Alcibiades: He should.

Socrates: At that time when it is better?

Alcibiades: Yes.

Socrates: And as much as is better?

Alcibiades: I say so.

B **Socrates:** What then? Since you used the term "better" for both—for accompanying a song with lyre playing and for wrestling—what do you call what's better in lyre playing, as I call what's better in wrestling "athletic"? What do you call it?

Alcibiades: I can't bring it to mind.

Socrates: Well, try to imitate me. For I answered, I suppose, that which is correct in every case, and that which comes about in accordance with the art[10] is, surely, correct. Or not?

Alcibiades: Yes, it is.

Socrates: And wasn't the art athletics?

Alcibiades: Why, of course.

C **Socrates:** And I said that what's better in wrestling is athletic.

Alcibiades: You did say that.

Socrates: And wasn't it beautifully said?

Alcibiades: It seems so to me.

Socrates: Come on, then, and tell me yourself—for, I suppose, it would be fitting for you too to speak beautifully[11]—first, what is the art of playing the lyre and singing and dancing correctly? What is it called all together? Are you still not able to say?

Alcibiades: Certainly not.

Socrates: Try it like this. Who are the goddesses of this art?

Alcibiades: Do you mean the Muses, Socrates?

D **Socrates:** I do. Look, what name does the art get from them?

Alcibiades: It seems to me that you mean "music."

---

[10] I use the traditional rendering of *technē*, "art," but it could also be translated as "skill," "craft," or "expertise." If you understand what you're doing, can explain your actions and your subject matter to others, and are not working merely by experience, you possess an art.

[11] A little joke: Alcibiades is beautiful (*kalos*), so should speak beautifully. The joke is rather more natural in Greek than in English, for *kalos* can also refer to excellence beyond aesthetics, in which case I will translate it as "admirable."

Socrates: That's what I mean. So what comes about correctly in accordance with this art? I was telling you about what turns out correctly in accordance with the art of athletics: what do you say in this case? How does it turn out?

Alcibiades: Musically, it seems to me.

Socrates: Well put. Come on, then, when it comes to "the better" both in waging war and in keeping peace, what term do you use for E this "better"? Just as in each case you said what was better, that it was the more musical in one, and in the other case the more athletic. Try to say what the better is here, too.

Alcibiades: Well, I can't quite say.

Socrates: But surely it is disgraceful[12] if, when you were speaking and giving advice about food, saying that this one was better than that, and at this time, and in such and such an amount, someone were to ask, "So what do you mean by 'better,' Alcibiades?" you were able to say that it was what was more healthy, although you do not claim to be a doctor. But when it comes to something 109A you claim to understand, and you will rise to give advice about as if you knew it, won't you be ashamed if, questioned about this, you can't—as is seems you can't—say anything? Won't this seem disgraceful?

Alcibiades: Of course.

Socrates: Then consider this and make an effort to say what "better" refers to in keeping peace and in making war with those one should.

Alcibiades: Even when I consider it I can't bring it to mind.

Socrates: Don't you know that whenever we make war we go off to fight blaming each other for some suffering, and that we name it as we go off?

B

Alcibiades: I do: we say we're being cheated of something, or being done some violence, or being deprived of something.

Socrates: Hold on: how is it that we've suffered each of these things? Try to say how one way differs from another.

Alcibiades: Do you mean, Socrates, whether it's justly or unjustly?

Socrates: That's exactly it.

Alcibiades: Why, that makes all the difference.

---

[12] *Aischros*, the Greek for "disgraceful" here, can also mean "ugly."

Socrates: What then? Which will you advise the Athenians to war against, those who are acting unjustly or those who are doing what is just?

C **Alcibiades:** You're asking a tricky question. For even if someone thinks that we should war against those who are doing what is just, he wouldn't admit it.

Socrates: For this is not customary,[13] it seems.

Alcibiades: Certainly not.

Socrates: Nor does it seem admirable.

<**Alcibiades:** No.>[14]

Socrates: So you also will make your arguments with regard to these things?

Alcibiades: Necessarily.

Socrates: So the "better" I was asking about just now with regard to waging war or not, and against whom one should and against whom one should not, and when and when not, is the more just. Or not?

Alcibiades: It appears so.

D **Socrates:** How's this, my friend Alcibiades? Were you unaware that you did not understand this, or did you learn and study with a teacher who taught you to recognize what's more just and what's more unjust without my being aware of it? And who is he? Point him out to me too, so that you can introduce me to him as a student as well.

Alcibiades: You're making fun of me, Socrates.

Socrates: No, by the god of friendship,[15] mine and yours, whom I would least of all forswear. But if you can, say who this teacher is.

E **Alcibiades:** And what if I can't? Don't you think I could know in some other way about what's just and what's unjust?

---

[13] The Greek *nomimos*, here rendered by "customary," can also mean "lawful."

[14] Alcibiades' reply seems to have been lost from our text, which has led many editors to assign the previous line to him. But the ancient commentators Proclus and Olympiodorus confirm the manuscripts' attribution of that line to Socrates, and Carlini's simple "No" is as good a guess as any for the missing reply.

[15] Zeus as god of friendship.

Socrates: Yes, at least if you were to discover it.

Alcibiades: But don't you believe I would discover it?

Socrates: Very much so, if you were to seek it out.

Alcibiades: Then don't you think I would seek it out?

Socrates: I do, at least if you were to believe you did not know.

Alcibiades: Then wasn't there a time when I was in that state?

Socrates: Beautifully put. Can you say, then, what this time was when you did not think that you knew what's just and what's unjust? 110A Come on, was it last year that were you seeking it out and didn't think you knew it? Or did you think you knew? And tell the truth when you answer, so our conversations don't turn out to be in vain.

Alcibiades: Well, I thought I knew.

Socrates: Didn't you think the same thing two and three and four years ago?

Alcibiades: I did.

Socrates: But before that you were a child. Weren't you?

Alcibiades: Yes.

Socrates: Well, I know well that you thought you knew then.

Alcibiades: How are you so sure?

B **Socrates:** Many times I listened to you at your teachers' and elsewhere, when you were a child, and when you were playing dice or some other childhood game you didn't act like one who was at a loss about what's just and what's unjust, but with a big, bold voice you'd say that whatever boy it happened to be was a wretch and unjust and was acting unjustly. Isn't that true?

Alcibiades: But what was I to do, Socrates, whenever someone treated me unjustly?

Socrates: What should you have done, you're saying, if you didn't know whether you were being treated unjustly or not then?

C **Alcibiades:** By Zeus, I did know, and I recognized clearly that I was being treated unjustly.

Socrates: So even as a child, it seems, you thought that you understood what's just and what's unjust.

Alcibiades: I did. And I did understand.

Socrates: At just what time did you discover it? For it wasn't, surely, when you thought you knew.

Alcibiades: Certainly not.

Socrates: So when did you believe that you were ignorant? Consider it—you won't discover that time.

Alcibiades: By Zeus, Socrates, I really can't say.

D **Socrates:** Then you do not know these things through discovering them yourself.

Alcibiades: I really don't seem to.

Socrates: But just now you said that you didn't know them through learning them, either. If you have neither discovered them nor learned them, how have you come to know them, and where?

Alcibiades: Well, perhaps I didn't answer you correctly when I said that I know these things through discovering them by myself.

Socrates: And how was that?

Alcibiades: I, too, learned, I think, like everyone else.

Socrates: We've come back to same the argument. From whom? Point him out to me, too.

E **Alcibiades:** From the many.[16]

Socrates: These are no serious teachers you've taken refuge with by giving credit to the many.

Alcibiades: What? Aren't they adequate teachers?

Socrates: Not even for teaching good and bad moves in checkers.[17] And this, I think, is a more trivial matter than what's just. What? Don't you think so?

Alcibiades: Yes.

Socrates: Then they are not able to teach more trivial things, but can teach more serious ones?

---

[16] Greek *hoi polloi.* "The many" or "most people" are the common people or general public. Protagoras similarly argues that most people have a sense of justice in the same way that they know Greek (*Protagoras* 327e–328b).

[17] Greek *petteia* is the general term for board games played with small pieces, sometimes along with dice. The game was said to require much skill, but it is often contrasted, in Plato, with the more important art being investigated.

Alcibiades: I myself think so. At least they're able to teach many things more serious than how to play checkers.

Socrates: What sorts of things?

111A **Alcibiades:** For example, I myself learned Greek from them. I couldn't tell you who my teacher was, but I give credit to those very people who you said were not serious teachers.

Socrates: Well, my noble fellow, the many are good teachers of this, and it would be only just for you to resort to their teaching.

Alcibiades: And why is that?

Socrates: Because when it comes to this they have what good teachers should have.

Alcibiades: What do you mean?

Socrates: Don't you know that those who are going to teach anything B should first know it themselves? Or not?

Alcibiades: Why, of course.

Socrates: And that those who know should agree with each other and not differ?

Alcibiades: Yes.

Socrates: When they differ about something, will you say that they know it?

Alcibiades: Certainly not.

Socrates: Then how could they be teachers of that?

Alcibiades: There's no way.

Socrates: What then? Do the many seem to you to differ about which C things are stones or sticks? If you ask anyone, don't they agree on the same things, and hurry to the same things, whenever they want to get a stone or a stick? It's the same way with everything else like this. For I pretty well understand that this is what you mean by understanding Greek. Or not?

Alcibiades: Yes.

Socrates: Now when it comes to this, as we've said, in private life they agree with each other and each as an individual agrees with himself, and in public cities do not dispute with each other, some saying one thing, others another.

Alcibiades: No, they don't.

Socrates: Then it's likely that they would be good teachers of these things, at any rate.

D **Alcibiades:** Yes.

Socrates: So if we wanted to make someone knowledgeable about these things, we would be correct to send him to the many for schooling?

Alcibiades: Of course.

Socrates: What if we wanted him to know not only which things are people, or which horses, but also which of them are good racers and which not? Would the many still be adequate teachers of this?

Alcibiades: Certainly not.

Socrates: And it is sufficient evidence for you that they do not understand E these things and are not "goodly teachers"[18] of them, since they do not agree at all with each other about them?

Alcibiades: For me it is.

Socrates: And what if we wanted to know, not only which things are people, but which people are healthy or sickly? Would the many have been adequate teachers for us?

Alcibiades: Certainly not.

Socrates: And it would be evidence for you that they are miserable teachers of these things, if you saw them disagreeing?

Alcibiades: For me it would.

Socrates: What about this? When it comes to just and unjust people 112A and deeds, do the many seem to you to agree with themselves or with each other?

Alcibiades: Least of all, by Zeus, Socrates.

Socrates: And do they differ about these things most?

Alcibiades: By far.

Socrates: Well, I think that you've never seen or heard of people differing enough with one another about what's healthy and what's not to fight and kill one another because of this.

Alcibiades: Certainly not.

Socrates: But when it comes to what's just and what's unjust I know B that, even if you haven't seen this, you have certainly heard it from Homer and many others. For you've heard the *Odyssey* and

---

[18] Probably a tag from a lost bit of poetry about bad teachers, which explains the rare word *krēguos* ("goodly").

the *Iliad*.[19]

Alcibiades: Surely, Socrates, by all means.

Socrates: Aren't these poems about a difference about what's just and what's unjust?

Alcibiades: Yes.

Socrates: And it's because of this difference that the Achaeans[20] and the Trojans had their battles and deaths, and Odysseus and the suitors of Penelope.

C **Alcibiades:** That's true.

Socrates: And I think that when it comes to those Athenians and Lacedaemonians and Boeotians who died at Tanagra, and those who died later at Coroneia—among whom your father Cleinias also met his end—their deaths and battles were produced by a difference about nothing other than justice and injustice.[21] Isn't that so?

Alcibiades: That's true.

Socrates: Are we then to say that they understood the things they D disagreed so strongly about that in their dispute they took the most extreme measures against each other?

Alcibiades: It doesn't appear so, at any rate.

Socrates: So aren't you giving credit to the sort of teachers that you yourself agree do not know?

Alcibiades: It's likely that I am.

Socrates: How, then, is it likely that you know what's just and what's unjust, when you are so confused about this and have clearly never learned it from anyone or discovered it yourself?

Alcibiades: From what you are saying, it's not likely.

E **Socrates:** Don't you see that once more you've not put this beautifully, Alcibiades?

Alcibiades: How's that?

Socrates: Because you say that I am saying these things.

---

[19] Alcibiades would have heard Homer recited, certainly in school and probably also by *rhapsodes* in public performance (for the latter, see Plato's *Ion*).

[20] "Achaeans" is one of the terms Homer uses for the Greeks.

[21] The Athenians were defeated by the Spartans and the Boeotians at Tanagra (458) and by the Boeotians at Coroneia (447).

Alcibiades: What? Isn't it you who are saying that I understand nothing about what's just and unjust?

Socrates: No, it isn't.

Alcibiades: Then it's me?

Socrates: Yes.

Alcibiades: How?

Socrates: You'll see. It's like this: if I ask you which is more, one or two, you'll say that it's two.

Alcibiades: I will.

Socrates: By how much?

Alcibiades: By one.

Socrates: So which of us is saying that two is one more than one?

Alcibiades: I am.

Socrates: Now I was asking, and you were answering?

Alcibiades: Yes.

113A **Socrates:** And when it comes to these things, is it clear that I, the one asking, am speaking, or is it you, the one answering?

Alcibiades: It's me.

Socrates: What if I asked how to spell "Socrates," and you told me? Which of us would be speaking?

Alcibiades: I would.

Socrates: Come on then, sum it up in a word. Whenever there is questioning and answering, which is the one speaking, the questioner or the answerer?

Alcibiades: The answerer is, Socrates, it seems to me.

B **Socrates:** Well, was I the questioner through all of this just now?

Alcibiades: Yes.

Socrates: And you the answerer?

Alcibiades: Of course.

Socrates: What then? Which of us said the things which were spoken?

Alcibiades: I would appear to be the one, Socrates, from what has been agreed.

Socrates: So it was said that Alcibiades the beautiful, the son of Cleinias, does not understand what's just and unjust, but thinks he does, and is about to go to the Assembly to advise the Athenians concerning things he knows nothing about. Wasn't that it?

C **Alcibiades:** It appears so.

Socrates: So the saying of Euripides holds, Alcibiades: you probably haven't heard these things from me, nor am I the one speaking, but it's you who are speaking, and you blame me in vain.[22] And yet you've said it well. For it is a mad undertaking you intend to take in hand, best of men, to teach what you do not know, having taken no care to learn it.

D **Alcibiades:** I think, Socrates, that the Athenians and the rest of the Greeks rarely deliberate about whether something is more just or more unjust. This sort of thing they believe to be clear, and so letting this be they consider which will be advantageous to those who do it. For what's just is not the same, I think, as what's advantageous, and many have profited from having unjustly done great injustice, while others, I think, have gotten no advantage from doing what's just.

E **Socrates:** What then? If what's just is really one thing, and what's advantageous something different, you can hardly think now that you know what's advantageous to people, and why, can you?

Alcibiades: What's stopping me, Socrates? Unless you're going to ask me again about who I learned it from or how I discovered it myself.

Socrates: This is really something! If you say anything that's not correct, and it so happens that is possible to prove this through the same argument as before, you think that novelties and different proofs must be heard, as if the previous ones were like worn-out bits

---

[22] In Euripides' *Hippolytus*, Phaedra's nurse is trying to find out what is wrong with her (350-352).

> **Nurse**: *What are you saying? Are you in love, my child? With whom?*
> **Phaedra**: *This man, whoever he is, the son of the Amazon . . .*
> **Nurse**: *Hippolytus, it's him you speak of?*
> **Phaedra**: *You hear this from yourself, not from me.*

Phaedra's claim obviously cannot be taken at face value, and if our author expected his readers to remember the Euripidean context, we are not to take Socrates' claim that only Alcibiades is speaking at face value either.

of clothing, and you wouldn't wear them any more, unless
114A someone brings you pure and immaculate evidence. I will let your preemptive strikes against the argument go, and will nonetheless ask you again where you learned your knowledge of what's advantageous, and who your teacher is, and all of those previous things I ask together in one question.

But it's clear that you will end up in the same place and will not be able to show how you know what's advantageous either by discovering it or by learning it. Since you're too spoiled for that, and would not enjoy tasting the same argument again, I'll let this go—whether you know, or don't know, what's advantageous for
B the Athenians. But why don't you prove whether the same things are both just and advantageous? If you'd like, ask me as I was asking you, or, if you like, go through the argument yourself on your own.

Alcibiades: Well, I don't know if I would be able, Socrates, to go through it for you.

Socrates: Well, my good man, consider me to be the Assembly and the people. There too, you know, you'll have to persuade each individual. Won't you?

Alcibiades: Yes.

Socrates: Now isn't the same person able to persuade individuals one
C by one and many together about whatever he knows, just as the grammarian, I suppose, persuades both one and many about letters?

Alcibiades: Yes.

Socrates: And won't the same person persuade both one and many about numbers?

Alcibiades: Yes.

Socrates: He will be the one who knows, the mathematician?

Alcibiades: Of course.

Socrates: Then you too are able to persuade one person about the same things you can persuade many about.

Alcibiades: That's likely.

Socrates: And it's clear that these things are the things you know.

Alcibiades: Yes.

Socrates: So this is the only difference between the orator in the Assembly
D and one in this sort of gathering: one persuades crowds about the same things, the other persuades individuals?

Alcibiades: Probably.

Socrates: Come on then, since it appears that the same person persuades many and one, practice on me and try to show that the just sometimes is not advantageous.

Alcibiades: You are hubristic, Socrates![23]

Socrates: Now, at any rate, it's because of hubris that I'm about to persuade you of the opposite of what you are not willing to persuade me.

Alcibiades: Speak on.

Socrates: Just answer the questions.

E **Alcibiades:** No, you speak by yourself.

Socrates: What? Don't you really want to be persuaded of this?

Alcibiades: Surely, by all means.

Socrates: And you'd really be persuaded if you said, "That's how it is"?

Alcibiades: So it seems to me.

Socrates: Answer then. And if you do not hear from yourself that what's just is also advantageous, don't believe anyone else saying it.

Alcibiades: No, I won't. So answer it is—since I don't think it will hurt any.

115A **Socrates:** You'd make a good diviner. Now tell me: you say that some just things are advantageous, and some are not?

Alcibiades: Yes.

Socrates: And some of them are admirable,[24] some not?

Alcibiades: What are you asking?

Socrates: If you have ever thought that someone has done something disgraceful but just.

---

[23] Hubris is a gratuitous attack on another's honor. For this sort of semijocular, conversational hubris compare *Symposium* 175e (Agathon of Socrates), 215b, 219c, and 222a (all Alcibiades of Socrates); *Meno* 76a (Socrates of Meno); and *Hippias Major* 286c (Socrates of the mystery man who refuted him).

[24] "Admirable" here again translates the ethical sense of *kalos*, which is also translated as "beautiful." "Disgraceful" in Socrates' next line is similarly used for *aischros*, which can also mean "ugly."

Alcibiades: No, I haven't.

Socrates: But all that is just is also admirable?

Alcibiades: Yes.

Socrates: Then what about what's admirable? Are all admirable things good, or are some good and others not?

Alcibiades: For my part, Socrates, I think that some of what's admirable is bad.

Socrates: And some disgraceful things are good?

Alcibiades: Yes.

B **Socrates:** Do you mean this sort of thing? Many in war, after coming to the aid of a comrade or relative, are wounded or die, while others, who do not aid them when they should, get off unhurt.[25]

Alcibiades: Definitely.

Socrates: So this sort of aid you call admirable with respect to the attempt to save those one should save, and this is courage. Or not?

Alcibiades: Yes.

Socrates: But you call it bad with respect to the deaths and wounds? Don't you?

Alcibiades: Yes.

C **Socrates:** Now isn't courage one thing, and death another?

Alcibiades: Of course.

Socrates: So aiding one's friends is not admirable and bad in the same respect?

Alcibiades: It doesn't appear so.

Socrates: Now look at it like this to see whether, at least inasmuch as it is admirable, it is also good. For you agree that aid is admirable with respect to courage. So consider this very thing, courage—is it good or bad?

Consider it like this: which would you choose for yourself, good things or bad?

Alcibiades: Good ones.

---

[25] The example is dramatically appropriate, as Socrates, at some risk to himself, would save Alcibiades' life at the battle of Potidaea, and Alcibiades would go some way toward returning the favor at Delium (*Symposium* 220d–221b).

D **Socrates:** And the greatest ones?

Alcibiades: Most of all.[26]

Socrates: And you would least of all choose to be deprived of such things?

Alcibiades: Why, of course.

Socrates: So what do you say about courage? At what price would you choose to be deprived of it?

Alcibiades: I would not choose even to live as a coward.

Socrates: Then cowardice seems to you to be the most extreme of bad things?

Alcibiades: To me it does.

Socrates: Equal to being dead, it seems.

Alcibiades: I say so.

Socrates: Now aren't life and courage most opposite to death and cowardice?

Alcibiades: Yes.

E **Socrates:** And the former you'd want most of all for yourself, and the latter the least?

Alcibiades: Yes.

Socrates: Because you believe the former are the best things, the latter the worst?

<**Alcibiades:** Of course.

Socrates: So you consider courage to be among the best of things, and death among the worst?>[27]

Alcibiades: I do.

Socrates: So coming to the aid of one's friends in war, inasmuch as it is admirable because it involves a good, courageous action, you call an admirable thing?

Alcibiades: I appear to.

Socrates: And inasmuch as it involves a bad, fatal action, you call it bad?

---

[26] I assign the *malista* of d1 to Alcibiades rather than introducing a reply for him.

[27] These lines, like those at 128a and 133c below, are not found in manuscripts of the *Alcibiades I*, but only in quotations from later authors.

Alcibiades: Yes.

Socrates: So it is just to address each of the actions like this. If you call it bad inasmuch as it accomplishes something bad, it must be called

116A good inasmuch as it accomplishes something good.

Alcibiades: It seems so to me.

Socrates: Then, too, inasmuch as it is good, it is admirable? And inasmuch as it is bad, it is disgraceful?

Alcibiades: Yes.

Socrates: So by saying that aiding friends in war is admirable, but bad, you are saying nothing different than if you said that it was good but bad?

Alcibiades: What you're saying seems to be true, Socrates.

Socrates: So nothing that is admirable, so far as it is admirable, is bad, nor is anything disgraceful, so far as it is disgraceful, good.

B **Alcibiades:** It does not appear so.

Socrates: Now consider it like this also. Isn't whoever is doing admirably also doing well?

Alcibiades: Yes.

Socrates: And aren't those who are doing well happy?

Alcibiades: Why, of course.

Socrates: Now, they are happy through the possession of good things?

Alcibiades: Most of all.

Socrates: And they possess them through doing well and admirably?

Alcibiades: Yes.

Socrates: So doing well is a good thing?

Alcibiades: Why, of course.

Socrates: And is doing good[28] admirable?

Alcibiades: Yes.

---

[28] "Doing good" translates *eupragia*, which has the same derivation as *eu prattein*, translated "do well" just above. I introduce "good" here because *eupragia* is more often used of altruistic acts, and thus helps Socrates identify the admirable (*kalon*) with the good (*agathon*).

C **Socrates:** So the same thing has appeared to us once again to be both admirable and good.

Alcibiades: It appears so.

Socrates: So whatever we discover to be admirable, we will also discover to be good, according to this argument at any rate?

Alcibiades: Necessarily.

Socrates: And are good things advantageous or not?

Alcibiades: They're advantageous.

Socrates: Do you remember what we agreed about what's just?

Alcibiades: I think it was that those who do what's just necessarily do something admirable.

Socrates: And that those who do what's admirable do something good?

Alcibiades: Yes.

D **Socrates:** And that good things are advantageous.

Alcibiades: Yes.

Socrates: So what's just, Alcibiades, is advantageous.

Alcibiades: It seems so.

Socrates: What then? Aren't you the speaker of these things, while I am the questioner?

Alcibiades: I appear to be, as it seems.

Socrates: So if someone stands up to advise the Athenians or the Peparethians,[29] thinking he knows what's just and what's unjust, and is going to say that what's just is sometimes bad, surely you'd E laugh at him, since you yourself are saying that the same things are both just and advantageous?

Alcibiades: By the gods, Socrates, I don't know what I'm saying myself, and I seem just like someone in a strange state. As you question me, at one time things seem one way, but at another time they seem different.

---

[29] Denyer (2001: 152) points out that Peparethos, an obscure island in the Aegean, was in the news in 361 B.C., and would date the dialogue soon after that date (i.e., rather late in Plato's career). Others cite a later event at Peparethos in 340, seven years after Plato's death. But perhaps the obscure island is just an obscure island, cited for its obscurity.

Socrates: Then, my friend, are you ignorant of what this condition is?

Alcibiades: Of course.

Socrates: Do you think that, if someone asked you whether you had two eyes or three, or two hands or four, or something else like this, you would give one answer at one time and another at another, or always the same?

117A **Alcibiades:** By this point I'm afraid about myself, but I think it would be the same.

Socrates: Is it because you know? Is this the cause?

Alcibiades: I think so, for my part.

Socrates: So when you unwillingly give opposite answers about things, it's clear you don't know about them?

Alcibiades: That's likely.

Socrates: Now concerning what's just and unjust, and admirable and disgraceful, and bad and good, and advantageous and not, don't you say that you are confused[30] as you give your answers? And isn't it clear that it's because you don't know about these things that you are confused?

B **Alcibiades:** To me it is.

Socrates: So is this how it is? Whenever someone doesn't know something, his soul is necessarily confused about it?

Alcibiades: Why, of course.

Socrates: What then? Do you know how to go up to the sky?[31]

Alcibiades: No, by Zeus, I do not.

Socrates: Is your opinion about this confused too?

Alcibiades: Certainly not.

Socrates: Do you know the cause, or shall I say?

Alcibiades: Say it.

---

[30] Forms of *planaomai* are here and elsewhere translated by "confused" and the like; the literal meaning of the Greek is closer to "wander." Compare our use of "ramble" (which, however, often won't work as a translation, as it implies some attempt at written or spoken expression). For Alcibiades' vacillation, compare *Gorgias* 481d–482b.

[31] "Going up to the sky" is what the Giants tried to do in their attempt to overthrow the Olympian gods.

Socrates: It's because, my friend, you don't think that you understand this when you don't understand it.

C **Alcibiades:** How do you mean this?

Socrates: Look at it in common with me. When you don't understand something, but recognize that you don't understand it, are you confused about that sort of thing? Like the preparation of gourmet food—you know, surely, that you do not know about this?

Alcibiades: Of course.

Socrates: Then do you have an opinion about how one should prepare these things and are you confused, or do you turn this over to one who understands?

Alcibiades: The latter.

Socrates: What about if you were sailing in a ship? Would you have an D opinion about whether the tiller should be moved in or out, and, since you don't know, would you be confused, or would you turn this over to the helmsman[32] and keep your peace?

Alcibiades: I'd turn it over to the helmsman.

Socrates: So you aren't confused about the things you don't know, so long as you know that you don't know them?

Alcibiades: I likely am not.

Socrates: Now are you aware that mistakes in action come through this sort of ignorance, that of the person who doesn't know but thinks he does know?

Alcibiades: Again, what do you mean by this?

Socrates: It's when we think we know what we're doing, I suppose, that we attempt to do something.

Alcibiades: Yes.

E **Socrates:** But some people, I suppose, when they do not think that they know, hand it over to others.

Alcibiades: Why, of course.

---

[32] The helmsman (*kubernētēs*) was second in command of an Athenian trireme if the trierarch (the aristocrat who had paid for the maintenance of the trireme for that year) was on board and was qualified to command a ship; otherwise the helmsman would be in charge. Alcibiades' final fall from grace came in 407 B.C. when he left his fleet in the hands of his friend and helmsman, Antiochus, only to have Antiochus fight a battle against Alcibiades' orders.

Socrates: So this sort of people who do not know live without making mistakes, since they turn it over to others to act concerning these things?

Alcibiades: Yes.

Socrates: So who are the people who make mistakes? It's not, I suppose, those who know.

Alcibiades: Certainly not.

Socrates: Since it is neither those who know nor those who don't know 118A but know that they do not know, are any others left, save those who don't know but think that they do?

Alcibiades: None other than these.

Socrates: So this ignorance is the cause of bad things and is the most contemptible stupidity?

Alcibiades: Yes.

Socrates: And when it's about the greatest things, then it does most harm and is most disgraceful?

Alcibiades: By far.

Socrates: What then? Can you name anything greater than what's just and admirable and what's good and what's advantageous?

Alcibiades: Certainly not.

Socrates: And isn't it about these things that you say you are confused?

Alcibiades: Yes.

Socrates: But if you are confused, isn't it clear from what came before B that not only are you ignorant of the greatest things, but not knowing them you think that you do know?

Alcibiades: Probably.

Socrates: Then alas, Alcibiades, what a condition you suffer from! I hesitate to name it, but, since we two are alone, it must be said. You are wedded to stupidity, best of men, of the most extreme sort, as the argument accuses you and you accuse yourself. So this is why you are leaping into the affairs of the city before you have been educated. You are not the only one to suffer from this; most of those who manage the affairs of the city are the same way, except C a few—perhaps including your guardian, Pericles.

Alcibiades: And you know, Socrates, he is said not to have become wise by chance, but by associating with many who are wise, including

Pythoclides and Anaxagoras. And even now at his age he associates with Damon for this very reason.[33]

Socrates: What then? Have you ever seen anyone wise who is unable to make someone else wise in his area of expertise? For example, the person who taught you to read was himself wise, and made you wise, and could do the same for whoever else he wished. Couldn't he?

Alcibiades: Yes.

D **Socrates:** Now you, too, the one who learned from him, could make another wise?

Alcibiades: Yes.

Socrates: And the same goes for the lyre player and the trainer?

Alcibiades: Of course.

Socrates: For this, surely, is admirable evidence that those who understand something do understand it, that they are able to produce someone else who understands it.

Alcibiades: It seems so to me.

Socrates: What then? Can you name anyone Pericles has made wise, starting with his own sons?

E **Alcibiades:** What if the sons of Pericles were both born fools, Socrates?[34]

Socrates: Well, what about your brother, Cleinias?[35]

Alcibiades: Why mention Cleinias, that madman?

---

[33] Socrates credits the philosopher Anaxagoras with helping Pericles add a certain elevated garrulousness to his oratory (*Phaedrus* 270a); Pericles' enemies are said to have charged Anaxagoras with impiety as a way of getting at Pericles. Socrates himself once looked to the philosopher Anaxagoras' doctrine of Mind for instruction, but was disappointed (*Phaedo* 97c–99d). Damon and Pythoclides were both sophists with special expertise in music. Damon advised Pericles on music and, perhaps, the radically democratic measure of paying jurors; he is said to have been ostracized. Socrates recommends him as a teacher in the *Laches* (180c–d).

[34] Pericles' sons are also characterized as underachievers at *Meno* 94b, *Protagoras* 319e–320a, and Aristotle *Rhetoric* 2.15 1390b27–31.

[35] At *Protagoras* 320a–b, Socrates notes that Pericles asked his brother Ariphron to raise Cleinias because he was worried Alcibiades would corrupt him, only to have Ariphron give up after six months and return Cleinias to Alcibiades. We know little else about him.

Socrates: Well, since Cleinias is mad, and the sons of Pericles were both born fools, what cause are we to assign in your case, to explain why Pericles overlooked you in your condition?

Alcibiades: I think that I am responsible myself because I did not put my mind to it.

119A **Socrates:** But tell me of another Athenian or foreigner, slave or free, who is reputed to have become wiser through associating with Pericles, as I can tell you that associating with Zeno has done for Pythodorus son of Isolochus and Callias son of Calliades, each of whom paid Zeno one hundred minas and became wise and famous.[36]

Alcibiades: By Zeus, I can't.

Socrates: Well, what do you intend for yourself? Will you go on as you are, or take care[37] of yourself?

B **Alcibiades:** Let's consider it in common, Socrates. And, you know, I'm aware of what you're saying and I agree. For those who manage the affairs of the city do seem, with a few exceptions, to be uneducated.

Socrates: And just what is the point of this?

Alcibiades: If they had been educated, I suppose, it would be necessary for one who was undertaking to compete against them to first learn and train as if he were going up against real athletes. But now, since they too go into the affairs of the city without any special skill, why should one train and bother oneself with learning? For C I know well that I will completely surpass them thanks to my nature.

Socrates: Alas, excellent man, what a thing you've said! How unworthy of your looks and your other advantages!

---

[36] The Zeno of paradox fame is sometimes clumped with the sophists (*Phaedrus* 261c), as he is here. Pythodorus hosts Parmenides and Zeno in Plato's *Parmenides*; he went on to be elected general at Athens, and to be exiled for corruption. This Callias would die as a general at Potidaea in 432 but may be meant to remind us of his namesake, the son of Hipponicus and brother-in-law of Alcibiades, who, if Socrates can be believed, spent more money on sophists than everyone else combined (*Apology* 20a). One hundred minas is a deliberate exaggeration of any fee a sophist could have charged at this time (see the note at 123c below).

[37] I regularly translate the Greek *epimeleia* and its cognates with some form of "care." The Greek carries connotations of effort, diligence, and attention rather than emotional attachment, and to take care of something, as we will see, does not mean merely to keep it safe but to improve it.

Alcibiades: Just what do you mean? Why say this, Socrates?

Socrates: I'm troubled on behalf of you and my love for you.

Alcibiades: How so?

Socrates: If you think it worthy that your competition be with the people here.

Alcibiades: But who should it be with?

D **Socrates:** This is certainly a worthy thing for a man who thinks he's so proud to come out and ask.

Alcibiades: What are you saying? Isn't my competition with these people?

Socrates: Well, if you had it in mind to take the helm of a trireme that was about to do battle, would it be enough for you to be the best of your fellow sailors when it came to seamanship, or would you think that this should be taken for granted, and look to your true antagonists, and not only, as now, to those who are competing on your side? You should, surely, so far surpass them that they not E think themselves worthy to compete against you, but, overawed by you, compete on your side against the enemy—if, that is, you do really have it in mind to accomplish something admirable and worthy of yourself and the city.

Alcibiades: But I do have that in mind.

Socrates: Then it's altogether worthy of you to be glad if you are the best common soldier, and not to look to the leaders of our opponents to see whether you have turned out better than they have, considering them and training with them in view.

120A **Alcibiades:** Who are these people you're talking about, Socrates?

Socrates: Don't you know that our city is always making war against the Lacedaemonians and the Great King?[38]

Alcibiades: That's true.

Socrates: So if you intend to be the leader of this city, you would be correct to believe that your competition is against the kings of the Lacedaemonians and the Persians?

Alcibiades: That's probably true.

---

[38] The king of Persia.

Socrates: Oh, no, my good man—you should look to Meidias the quail B raiser[39] and others like him, who attempt to manage the affairs of the city when they still have slavish hair on their souls,[40] as the women would say, and thanks to their lack of cultivation have not yet lost it. Still speaking their barbarian babble they come forward to suck up to the city, not to lead it. It's these, the ones I'm talking about, that you should look to, neglecting yourself. No, you shouldn't learn what can be learned when you are about to compete in such a competition, nor train where one must train, C but prepare all your preparations just as you have been and go into the affairs of the city just like this.

Alcibiades: Well, Socrates, what you're saying seems to me to be true, and yet I think that the generals of the Lacedaemonians and the king of the Persians are no different from the others.

Socrates: But, excellent man, consider what sort of belief this is.

Alcibiades: About what?

Socrates: First, do you think you would take more care of yourself if D you feared them and thought that they were dangerous, or if you thought they were not?

Alcibiades: Clearly if I believed they were dangerous.

Socrates: Now you don't believe that you would be harmed if you took care of yourself?

Alcibiades: Not at all—I'd be greatly helped.

Socrates: So your belief is quite bad in this respect.

Alcibiades: That's true.

---

[39] Meidias, an Athenian politician, was a popular butt of the comic poets (Aristophanes, *Birds* 1297–1299), who charged him with sycophancy and embezzlement, among other things. He raised quails for the curious sport of quail striking, in which one (human) player attempts to drive his opponent's bird from a circle by striking it with a finger upon its head. Alcibiades probably played the sport himself. Plutarch (*Life of Alcibiades* 10) tells us that Alcibiades accidentally released a quail from his cloak during his first speech before the Assembly. The quail was rescued by Antiochus, who would go on to be Alcibiades' helmsman and lose the battle of Notium for him: see Introduction, Section 2, and the note at 117d.

[40] Slaves had to keep their hair cut short, the better to do menial labor and to show off the tattoo that many were given on their foreheads. Thus here losing one's slavish hair ought to mean allowing one's hair to grow out. Alcibiades wore his own hair luxuriously long.

Socrates: Consider the second point, that it is false, judging by what's likely.

Alcibiades: How so?

Socrates: Is it likely that better natures will come to be in noble races, E or in ones that aren't noble?

Alcibiades: Clearly in noble ones.

Socrates: Now those who are born well, if they are also brought up well, will in this way likely turn out to be complete with regard to excellence?[41]

Alcibiades: Necessarily.

Socrates: Let's first consider, then, by comparing our situation to theirs, whether the kings of the Lacedaemonians and Persians seem to be of lesser lines than we are. Or don't we know that the former are descended from Heracles, the latter from Achaemenes, and that the lines of Heracles and Achaemenes go back to Perseus, son of Zeus?[42]

121A **Alcibiades:** And my line, Socrates, goes back to Eurysakes,[43] and that of Eurysakes to Zeus.

Socrates: And mine, my noble Alcibiades, goes back to Daedalus, and that of Daedalus to Hephaestus, son of Zeus.[44] But their lines, starting from themselves, have been kings who were sons of kings, all the way back to Zeus—kings of Argos and Lacedaemon in one case, in the other case kings of Persia always, and often, as now, of

---

[41] The Greek *aretē*, elsewhere often translated as "virtue", is here always rendered by "excellence." *Aretē* is that quality which makes anything a good example of its kind; it may, but need not, have a moral connotation.

[42] Both royal lines of Sparta claimed descent from Heracles; Achaemenes founded the Achaemenid dynasty that ruled Persia until Alexander the Great. To make the two lines seem more similar, Socrates plays up the rather tenuous connection each had to Zeus, through Perseus. Perseus was the great-grandfather of Heracles (who was himself a son of Zeus, of course, a far closer connection); Perseus' son Perses was the mythological ancestor of all of the Persians, and thus presumably of Achaemenes as well.

[43] The legendary Eurysakes, son of Ajax, son of Aeacus, son of Zeus, was said to have been king of Salamis before ceding it to Athens.

[44] Socrates, the son of a sculptor, parodies Alcibiades' tenuous claim to divine ancestry by claiming descent from the master artist Daedalus, who in some accounts was descended from the craftsman god Hephaestus. Compare *Euthyphro* 11b–c.

Asia as well. We ourselves are private citizens, as were our fathers. B And if you had to point out your ancestors or the ancestral land of Eurysakes, Salamis, or that of Aeacus before him, Aegina, to Artaxerxes,[45] son of Xerxes, how much do you think he'd laugh? Look out that we not prove to be worse off than these men both in the dignity of our lines and in our upbringing as well.

Haven't you observed how great the advantages of the kings of the Lacedaemonians are, whose wives are publicly guarded by the ephors in order that, as far as is possible, no one escape their notice and become king who has been born to someone other than C a descendant of Heracles?[46] The king of the Persians is so superior that there is no one who suspects that the next king might be the son of anyone other than him. For this reason the wife of the king is guarded by nothing other than fear. When the eldest child is born, he who will rule,[47] first all the subjects in the territory ruled by the king hold a festival, and then for the rest of time on the birthday of the king all of Asia holds royal sacrifices and feasts. D When we are born, as the comic poet put it,[48] even the neighbors hardly notice anything, Alcibiades.

After this the boy is raised not by some worthless woman nurse, but by the eunuchs who are thought to be the best of those in the king's service. To these are given the task of caring for the newborn child, and in order to contrive that he turn out to be

---

[45] Salamis and Aegina are fairly small islands visible from Athens. Artaxerxes, king of Persia from 465 to 424, would have scoffed at their size, but would also have remembered the disastrous defeat Xerxes' fleet suffered off Salamis in 480.

[46] Anachronistic irony. Alcibiades was widely believed to have had an affair with the wife of the Spartan king Agis about twenty years after the dramatic date of the dialogue; she then gave birth to an illegitimate son. The ephors were elected Spartan officials with wide power over domestic affairs.

[47] The Persian succession was in practice rather less regular than this. Artaxerxes had killed his older brother; his son Ochus (Darius II) would kill two brothers before securing the throne for himself; and his heir, another Artaxerxes, would face a rebellion from the Cyrus who had led Persian forces against Athens and Alcibiades in the Peloponnesian War. It is this rebellion that Xenophon would assist: see the note at 123b below.

[48] The comic poet Plato, a contemporary of Alcibiades (and no relation to the philosopher), fragment 204 Kock. The line became proverbial, but its original context is lost.

most beautiful, they shape and straighten the child's limbs.[49] And
E for doing these things they are held in high esteem.

When the boys enter their seventh year, they turn to horses and riding instructors, and begin to go hunting. When the boy enters his fourteenth year, those who are called the royal tutors take him over. These are the four Persians selected because they have been deemed to be the best among those in their prime: the wisest man, the most just man, the most moderate man, and the
122A most courageous man. The first of these teaches the craft of the Magi, that of Zoroaster, son of Horomazus[50] (this consists of service to the gods), and he also teaches him about being a king. The most just man teaches him to tell the truth throughout his life; the most moderate man teaches him not to be ruled by any pleasure, so that he may be accustomed to be free and truly royal, since he rules first of all over the things within him, and is no slave to them. The most courageous man teaches by preparing him to be fearless
B and without dread, since to be afraid is to be a slave.

But in your case, Alcibiades, Pericles chose as your tutor the slave who was the most useless due to his age, Zopyrus the Thracian. I'd go through the rest of the upbringing and education of your competitors for you, if it weren't such a lot of work, and these things weren't sufficient to make clear the rest, which follows from them. Your breeding, Alcibiades, and your upbringing and education, or that of any other Athenian, is of concern, practically speaking, to no one—unless someone happens to love you.

C If you wish to look to riches and luxuries and fashion and trailing robes and ointments of myrrh and multitudes of slaves in attendance and the rest of the delicacies of the Persians,[51] you'd be ashamed of yourself, when you sensed how far you were left behind by them. And if you will wish to look to the moderation

---

49 Such bending of infants' limbs was also a common practice among the Greeks (*Republic* 2.377c, *Laws* 7.789c–e).

50 Zoroaster, dated by modern scholars to 1400–1200 B.C., founded the religion named after him. Its primary divinities were the god Ahuramazda (Greek Horomazus) and his evil counterpart, whose name means "the Lie": hence the emphasis on truth-telling in Persian culture. By the dramatic date of our dialogue the kings of Persia were probably Zoroastrians. The Magi were the priests of the Medes and hence of their Persian rulers. Socrates here mistakenly makes Horomazus Zoroaster's father, as happens elsewhere in our Greek sources.

51 Alcibiades would be fond of luxuries, including extravagant clothing. Plutarch (*Life of Alcibiades* 16.1) describes his "effeminate garments of purple dragged through the market-places."

and orderliness, the composure, contentedness, high-mindedness, discipline, courage, endurance, love of labor, love of victory, and love of honor of the Lacedaemonians, you'd believe yourself a mere child in all such things.

D And if you pay attention to wealth, and believe you are something special when it comes to this, we'll not leave even this unsaid in the hope that you may see where you stand. If you wish to look to the riches of the Lacedaemonians, you'll recognize that the riches here fall far short of those there. For no one here could rival all the land they hold, both their own and that in Messenia, either in size or excellence, nor in their possession of slaves, both helots[52] and the others, nor, surely, of horses or the other animals E that graze in Messenia. All this I'll let go, but there is not as much gold and silver among the rest of the Greeks as there is in private hands in Lacedaemon. For it has been going in for many generations now from all of the Greeks, and often also from the 123A barbarians, but it never comes out. It's just like the tale of Aesop that the fox told to the lion: the tracks of the money going into Lacedaemon are clear, but no one has ever seen the tracks coming out.[53] So one must know well that the people there are the richest of the Greeks in gold and silver, and the king is the richest of those there. For the kings receive the greatest shares of gold and silver, and most frequently, and the royal tribute the Lacedaemonians pay their kings is not small.

B The Lacedaemonians' wealth is great by Greek standards, but compared to the riches of the Persians and their king, it's nothing. I once heard from a trustworthy man, who was one of those who had gone up to see the king, that he had passed through a very large and good land, nearly a day's journey across, which the

---

[52] The Spartans had reduced their neighbors in Messenia (and some of the inhabitants of Laconia) to a servile status. Unlike chattel slaves, these helots reproduced in family groups and had some property rights, but they were themselves property of the Spartan state, and bitterly resented Spartan rule. Plato elsewhere characterizes the Spartans' treatment of the helots as impracticably harsh (*Laws* 6.777c–778a).

[53] An elderly lion is no longer able to go out and hunt, and pretends to be sick so that the other animals will come to see if this is the case; the fox notices that none of the visitors ever return (Halm 246 = Perry 142). Private possession of gold or silver coinage was illegal at Sparta, but this apparently didn't prevent the Spartans from corruption, especially after their victory in the Peloponnesian War in 404 B.C. gave them wider opportunities to enrich themselves overseas.

inhabitants called the girdle of the king's wife.[54] And there was C another that they called her veil, and many other beautiful and good regions reserved for the apparel of his wife, each place taking its name from some type of apparel.

Thus I think that if someone were to tell the mother of the king, and wife of Xerxes, Amestris,[55] that the son of Deinomache had it in mind to challenge her son— Deinomache, whose apparel is worth fifty minas, if that, and whose son has not even three hundred plethra of land in Erchiae[56]—she would wonder just what D this Alcibiades fellow is putting his trust in when he intends to vie with Artaxerxes. And I think she'd say that there's nothing else for this man to trust in as he makes his attempt other than care and wisdom, for these are the only noteworthy things among the Greeks. And if she learned that Alcibiades here who is now making his attempt has, first of all, barely entered his twentieth year; next that he is completely uneducated; and, furthermore, that when the one who loves him tells him that he must first learn and take E care of himself and train, and only then go to vie with the king, he is unwilling, but says he's content just as he is, I think she'd be amazed and ask, "Then just what does the lad put his trust in?" If we said that it was in his beauty and height and family and wealth and the nature of his soul, she'd believe, Alcibiades, that we were mad as she looked to their advantages in such things.

124A And I think that Lampido, the daughter of Leotychides, wife of Archidamus, and mother of Agis,[57] kings all of them, would be

---

[54] The man was perhaps Xenophon, who says that while he was a member of Cyrus' army and marching against King Artaxerxes he camped by a place whose revenues provided the queen with her girdle (*Anabasis* 1.4).

[55] Herodotus (9.108–113) and Ctesias (fragment 14) relate tales in which Amestris appears powerful and cruel. The Greeks often made the Persians out to be effeminate, as in the artistic convention in which Amazons stand in for Persians, and they were both intrigued and repelled by what they saw as the harem intrigue of the Persian court.

[56] Three hundred plethra are roughly seventy modern acres. The estate in Erchiae would have been worth a little more than four talents; four talents or so made one eligible for the special taxes levied against the rich at Athens. There are sixty minas in a talent, so Deinomache's fifty-mina wardrobe is also rather extensive. But compared to the fabulous wealth of the Persians, these respectable Athenian fortunes are puny.

[57] Leotychides was king of Sparta 491–469, Archidamus 469–427; Agis would be king 427–399.

amazed herself when looking to their advantages, if you intended to vie with her son despite being so badly brought up.

And don't you think it's disgraceful, if even the women of our enemies have a better idea of what sort of men we'd have to be to take them on than we do ourselves? Rather, you blessed B man, be persuaded by me and the inscription at Delphi: Know Thyself—recognize that these are your opponents, not those you think. We will surpass not even one of them, if not through care and art. If you fall short of them, you will fall short of becoming a name among the Greeks and barbarians, something you seem to me to love as no one has ever loved anything else.

Alcibiades: How must I take care of myself, then, Socrates? Can you explain it? For you really seem like one who's spoken the truth.

Socrates: Yes, I can. Or, rather, we must consider in common how we C can become the best possible. For, you know, I'm not saying that you must be educated, while I don't need to be, since I don't differ from you except in one way.

Alcibiades: What?

Socrates: My guardian is better and wiser than your guardian Pericles.

Alcibiades: Who is your guardian, Socrates?

Socrates: The god, Alcibiades, who did not allow me to speak with you before this day. It's him that I trust in when I say that your glory will come to light through no one else save me.

D **Alcibiades:** You're joking, Socrates.

Socrates: Perhaps. But I'm saying the truth when I say that we need to take care of ourselves, or rather that all people do, but the two of us very much indeed.

Alcibiades: About me you're not wrong.

Socrates: Nor about me.

Alcibiades: What are we to do, then?

Socrates: We must not give up or slack off, my companion.

Alcibiades: That would hardly be fitting, Socrates.

Socrates: No, it wouldn't, so we must consider this in common. And E tell me: we do say that we want to be as good as possible. Isn't that it?

Alcibiades: Yes.

Socrates: What sort of excellence are we aiming for?

Alcibiades: Clearly, that of men, good ones.

Socrates: Good at what?

Alcibiades: Clearly, those good at managing affairs.

Socrates: What sort of affairs? Those having to do with horses?

Alcibiades: Certainly not.

Socrates: For we would go to those skilled about horses?

Alcibiades: Yes.

Socrates: Then do you mean affairs having to do with ships?

Alcibiades: No.

Socrates: For we would go to those skilled about ships?

Alcibiades: Yes.

Socrates: Then what sorts of affairs? Those managed by whom?

Alcibiades: By Athenians who are admirable and good.[58]

125A **Socrates:** By the admirable and good do you mean those who are sensible[59] or those who are foolish?

Alcibiades: Those who are sensible.

Socrates: Now isn't each good at whatever he is sensible about?

Alcibiades: Yes.

Socrates: And wretched at what he is foolish about?

Alcibiades: Why, of course.

Socrates: So the cobbler is sensible when it comes to the making of shoes?

Alcibiades: Of course.

Socrates: So he's good at that?

Alcibiades: Yes, he's good.

Socrates: And isn't the cobbler foolish about making clothing?

Alcibiades: Yes.

---

[58] "Admirable and good" is a literal translation of *kaloi kagathoi*, a phrase with both ethical and class implications, which could also be rendered by "gentlemen" or "the better sort."

[59] *Phronein*, the word translated here and below as "sensible," can also be rendered as "prudent" or even "wise"; so also for cognates. See *Alcibiades II* 138c with note.

B **Socrates:** So he's bad at that?

Alcibiades: Yes.

Socrates: So according to this argument, at any rate, the same person is both bad and good.

Alcibiades: It appears so.

Socrates: Then do you say that good men are also bad?

Alcibiades: Certainly not.

Socrates: Well, just who do you say is good?

Alcibiades: I say it's those who are able to rule in the city.

Socrates: Not, surely, those able to rule horses?

Alcibiades: Certainly not.

Socrates: But people?

Alcibiades: Yes.

Socrates: Sick ones?

Alcibiades: No.

Socrates: Those who are sailing?

Alcibiades: That's not what I say.

Socrates: Those who are harvesting?

Alcibiades: No.

C **Socrates:** Well, is it those who are doing nothing or doing something?

Alcibiades: I mean those doing something.

Socrates: Doing what? Try to clarify it for me.

Alcibiades: It's those who do business with each other and make use of each other as we do in living in cities.

Socrates: So you're talking about ruling people who make use of other people?

Alcibiades: Yes.

Socrates: Is it coxswains who make use of rowers?

Alcibiades: Certainly not.

Socrates: For that would be the excellence of the helmsman?

Alcibiades: Yes.

D **Socrates:** Then do you mean people who rule the aulos players who lead people in song and make use of the members of the chorus?[60]

Alcibiades: Certainly not.

Socrates: For that would be the excellence of the director?

Alcibiades: Of course.

Socrates: So just what do you mean by being able to rule people who make use of people?

Alcibiades: I mean those who have a share in citizenship and who do business with each other—it's being able to rule these people in the city.

Socrates: So what art is this? Just as if I again asked you the same question I did just now—what art makes one understand how to rule those who have a share in sailing?

Alcibiades: That of the helmsman.

E **Socrates:** And what form of knowledge enables one to rule those who share in the song, as was said just now?

Alcibiades: The one you just said, that of the director.

Socrates: And what do you call the knowledge about those who share in citizenship?

Alcibiades: I call it good advice, Socrates.

Socrates: What? The advice helmsmen give doesn't seem bad, does it?

Alcibiades: Certainly not.

Socrates: But it's good advice?

126A **Alcibiades:** To me it seems so, good at least for keeping those who are sailing safe.

Socrates: Beautifully put. And the good advice you're talking about, what is it for?

Alcibiades: For running the city better and keeping it safe.

Socrates: And it is run better and kept safe by the presence or absence of what? Just as if you were to ask me, "The body is run better and kept safe through the presence or absence of what?" I'd say

[60] An aulos player provided musical accompaniment for Greek plays and their choruses. On the aulos see 106e with note.

B that it's when health is present and disease absent. Don't you think that's how it is?

Alcibiades: Yes.

Socrates: And if you asked me, "Eyes are better when what is present?" I'd say, in the same way, when sight is present, and blindness absent. And ears, when deafness is absent and hearing present, become better and are better tended.

Alcibiades: That's correct.

C **Socrates:** Well, what of this? A city becomes better and is better tended and run whenever what is present or absent?

Alcibiades: It seems to me, Socrates, that whenever there's friendship among the people for each other, and hatred and factional strife are absent.

Socrates: Now by friendship do you mean agreement[61] or disagreement?

Alcibiades: Agreement.

Socrates: Now through what art do cities agree about numbers?

Alcibiades: Mathematics.

Socrates: And what about private citizens? Isn't it through the same one?

Alcibiades: Yes.

D **Socrates:** And each person with himself?

Alcibiades: Yes.

Socrates: Through what art does each person agree with himself about whether a foot or a yard is longer? Isn't it through the art of measurement?

Alcibiades: Why, surely.

Socrates: And also private citizens and cities with each other?

Alcibiades: Yes.

Socrates: And isn't it the same when it comes to weight?

---

[61] The Greek *homonoia*, translated throughout by "agreement," can refer to intellectual agreement (the meaning Socrates seems to rely on) or emotional concord (which may be more what Alcibiades has in mind: see 126e). Factional strife (*stasis*) was common in many Greek cities, and agreement, particularly agreement about who was to rule, was thus a major goal of Greek politics.

Alcibiades: I say so.

Socrates: Now the agreement you're talking about, what is it and what's it about? What art produces it? And is it the same for a city and for a private citizen, both himself with himself and with another?

Alcibiades: That does seem likely.

E **Socrates:** So what is it? Don't grow weary of answering, but make an effort to speak.

Alcibiades: I think I mean the friendship and agreement that a father who loves his son shares with the son, as does the mother, and a brother with brother and wife with husband.

Socrates: Do you think, Alcibiades, that a husband[62] would be able to agree with his wife about spinning wool, he who does not understand it with she who does understand?

Alcibiades: Certainly not.

Socrates: Nor is there any need. For this, at any rate, is a subject for women to learn.

Alcibiades: Yes.

127A **Socrates:** And would a wife be able to agree with her husband about soldiering, when she hasn't learned about it?

Alcibiades: Certainly not.

Socrates: For this, at any rate, you would probably say is for men.

Alcibiades: I would.

Socrates: So some subjects of learning are for women, and some for men, according to your argument.

Alcibiades: Why, of course.

Socrates: So in these matters, at any rate, there is no agreement for wives with their husbands.

Alcibiades: No.

Socrates: So there's not any friendship, either, if indeed friendship is agreement.

Alcibiades: It appears not.

---

[62] The Greek *anēr*, translated here and below by "husband," is also the regular word for a man as opposed to a woman; so too the Greek *gunē* can mean both "wife" and "woman."

Socrates: So inasmuch as women do their own work,[63] their husbands are not friends to them.[64]

B **Alcibiades:** It's not likely.

Socrates: Nor are wives friends to their husbands, inasmuch as their husbands do their own work.

Alcibiades: No.

Socrates: Neither, then, are cities well run in this way, whenever everyone does their own work.

Alcibiades: I think they are, Socrates.

Socrates: What do you mean, if friendship is not present, and we said that cities were well run when it was present, and otherwise not?

Alcibiades: But it seems to me that it's just because of this, because each person does his own work, that friendship is present in cities.

C **Socrates:** It didn't a moment ago. But what do you mean now? Is friendship present when agreement isn't? Or is it possible for there to be agreement about something that some know and some do not?

Alcibiades: That's impossible.

Socrates: And are they doing what's just or what's unjust, when they do their own work?

Alcibiades: Why, what's just, of course.

Socrates: So when citizens in the city are doing what's just, friendship doesn't come to exist between them?

Alcibiades: To me it seems necessary that it come to exist, Socrates.

D **Socrates:** So just what is this friendship or agreement about which you say we must become wise and give good advice, if we are to become good men? I can learn neither what it is nor in whom it is present. Sometimes it appears to be present in the same people, sometimes not, at least from your argument.

---

[63] "Do their own work" (*ta hauton prattousin*) could also be rendered as "mind their own business"; it is one of the definitions of justice in the *Republic* (4.433a).

[64] The Greek for friendship (*philia*) is cognate with the verb here (*philein*), which is often translated "to love." Hence an alternative translation: "wives are not loved by their husbands." So also for Socrates' next line.

Alcibiades: By the gods, Socrates, I myself don't know what I'm saying, and I've probably been in the most disgraceful way for a long time without noticing it.

Socrates: Well, you must take heart. If you sensed that you were in this E state at fifty, it would be a difficult thing to take care of yourself. But now you're at the age when one ought to sense this.

Alcibiades: So what should one who senses this do, Socrates?

Socrates: Answer the questions, Alcibiades. And if you do this, God willing—if one should at all trust in my divining—both you and I will be better off.

Alcibiades: That's how it will be, at least as far as my answering goes.

128A **Socrates:** Come on then, what is it to take care of oneself—lest we without noticing it are perhaps not caring for ourselves when we think that we are—and when is it that one does this? When one takes care of the things that belong to him, does he then also take care of himself?

Alcibiades: It seems so to me, at any rate.

Socrates: And when does a person take care of his feet? Does he take care of them whenever he takes care of the things that belong to the feet?

Alcibiades: I don't understand.

Socrates: Do you speak of things belonging to the hand? For example, would you say that the ring belongs to any other part of a person than the finger?

Alcibiades: Certainly not.

Socrates: And a shoe to the foot in the same way?

Alcibiades: Yes.

<**Socrates:** And clothing and blankets likewise belong to the rest of the body?

B **Alcibiades:** Yes.>[65]

Socrates: So when we take care of shoes, are we then taking care of feet?

Alcibiades: I don't entirely understand, Socrates.

---

65 These lines, like those at 115e and 133c, are found only in quotations from later authors.

Socrates: What, Alcibiades? Do you speak of a correct way of taking care of any given thing?

Alcibiades: I do.

Socrates: Now, whenever someone makes something better, do you say this is correct care?

Alcibiades: Yes.

Socrates: So what art improves shoes?

Alcibiades: Cobbling.

Socrates: So we take care of shoes with cobbling?

C **Alcibiades:** Yes.

Socrates: Do we take care of feet with cobbling? Or by that art with which we make feet better?

Alcibiades: The latter.

Socrates: And we make the feet better with the same art with which we make the rest of the body better?

Alcibiades: It seems so to me.

Socrates: Isn't that athletics?

Alcibiades: Most certainly.

Socrates: So with athletics we take care of the foot, but with cobbling we take care of the things that belong to the foot?

Alcibiades: Of course.

Socrates: And by athletics we take care of the hands, but by ring-making, the things that belong to the hand?

Alcibiades: Yes.

Socrates: And by athletics we take care of the body, but by weaving D and the other arts, the things belonging to the body?

Alcibiades: By all means.

Socrates: So it's by one art that we take care of each thing itself, and by another one that we take care of the things that belong to it?

Alcibiades: It appears so.

Socrates: So whenever you take care of the things that belong to you, you are not taking care of yourself.

Alcibiades: By no means.

Socrates: For one doesn't use the same art, it's likely, to take care of oneself and the things that belong to one.

Alcibiades: It appears not.

Socrates: Come on, then, with what art could we take care of ourselves?

Alcibiades: I can't say.

E **Socrates:** But this much, at any rate, has been agreed: it's not the art we use to make anything at all of the things that belong to us better, but that which we use to make ourselves better.

Alcibiades: That's true.

Socrates: Now would we ever have recognized what art makes a shoe better if we didn't know what a shoe was?

Alcibiades: That's impossible.

Socrates: Nor what art makes rings better, if we were ignorant of what a ring was.

Alcibiades: True.

Socrates: And what art makes *oneself* better—could we ever know this if we were ignorant of just what we ourselves are?

129A **Alcibiades:** That's impossible.

Socrates: Then is it easy to know oneself, and was it some simpleton who inscribed this on the temple at Delphi, or is it difficult and not a matter for just anyone?

Alcibiades: To me, Socrates, it has often seemed to be a matter for anyone, but has often seemed most difficult.

Socrates: Well, Alcibiades, whether it is easy or not, nevertheless this is how it stands for us: if we knew this we could perhaps recognize what care of ourselves is, but in ignorance of this we never could.

Alcibiades: That's so.

B **Socrates:** Come on, in what way could the self itself[66] be discovered? For in this way we could perhaps discover just what we are ourselves, but if we remain in ignorance of it we'll be unable to do so, I suppose.

Alcibiades: You're correct.

Socrates: By Zeus, hold on—with whom are you conversing now? Surely it's with me?

---

[66] Others (as Denyer 2001) would render *auto to auto* here and at 130d as "the itself itself."

Alcibiades: Yes.

Socrates: And I with you?

Alcibiades: Yes.

Socrates: So Socrates is the one conversing?

Alcibiades: Of course.

Socrates: And Alcibiades the one listening?

Alcibiades: Yes.

Socrates: Now, doesn't Socrates converse through speech?

C **Alcibiades:** Why, surely.

Socrates: And you call conversing and making use of speech the same thing, I suppose.

Alcibiades: Of course.

Socrates: And the one who is using and what's being used, aren't they are different?

Alcibiades: What do you mean?

Socrates: Well, a cobbler cuts, I suppose, with a cutter and a knife and other tools.

Alcibiades: Yes.

Socrates: So the one who cuts and uses is one thing, and what he uses to cut is another.

Alcibiades: Why, of course.

Socrates: And just so the lyre player himself is something different from the things he plays with?

Alcibiades: Yes.

D **Socrates:** Well, this is what I was asking just now, if the one who uses and what he uses always seem to be different.

Alcibiades: It seems so.

Socrates: What, then, are we to say about the cobbler? Does he cut only with his tools, or also with his hands?

Alcibiades: Also with his hands.

Socrates: So he uses them too?

Alcibiades: Yes.

Socrates: Does he also make use of his eyes when he cuts?

Alcibiades: Yes.

Socrates: And we agree that the one using and the things he uses are different?

Alcibiades: Yes.

Socrates: So the cobbler and the lyre player are different from the hands E and eyes with which they work.

Alcibiades: It appears so.

Socrates: Now doesn't man[67] make use of his whole body?

Alcibiades: Of course.

Socrates: And what uses and what is used by it are different?

Alcibiades: Yes.

Socrates: So man is something different from his own body?

Alcibiades: It seems so.

Socrates: Then just what is man?

Alcibiades: I can't say.

Socrates: Well, you can say this, at any rate, that man is that which uses the body.

Alcibiades: Yes.

130A **Socrates:** Now, does something other than soul use it?

Alcibiades: Nothing else.

Socrates: By ruling it?

Alcibiades: Yes.

Socrates: And surely this, I think, no one would think otherwise about.

Alcibiades: What?

Socrates: That man is one of three things.

Alcibiades: Which?

Socrates: Soul or body or both together, this whole thing.

---

[67] In this passage (through 130c), I translate *anthrōpos*, which is usually "person" or "one" elsewhere, with the generic "man." "Man" elsewhere usually translates *anēr*, which explicitly marks a man as distinct from a woman.

Alcibiades: Why, surely.

Socrates: But we agreed that man was the very thing that ruled the body.

B **Alcibiades:** We did agree.

Socrates: Then does the body itself rule itself?

Alcibiades: By no means.

Socrates: Since we say it is ruled.

Alcibiades: Yes.

Socrates: So this wouldn't be what we are seeking.

Alcibiades: It's not likely.

Socrates: Then do both together rule the body, and is this what man is?

Alcibiades: Quite possibly.

Socrates: This least of all. For if one isn't sharing the rule, there's no way, I suppose, for both together to rule.

Alcibiades: Correct.

C **Socrates:** And since neither the body nor both together are man, then what remains, I think, is either that man is nothing, or, if man is something, he turns out to be nothing other than soul.

Alcibiades: Just so.

Socrates: So is there still any need to show you more clearly that the soul is man?

Alcibiades: No, by Zeus, this seems to me to be sufficient.

Socrates: And if it is not precise, but just within measure, that will suffice for us. For we will know this precisely whenever we discover the D thing we passed by just now because it would require so much investigation.

Alcibiades: What's that?

Socrates: What was said just now in pretty much these terms, that first the self itself must be investigated. Now instead of it we were investigating what each individual is. And perhaps this will suffice. For there's nothing, I suppose, that we would say is more authoritative over us than the soul.

Alcibiades: Certainly not.

Socrates: So this would be an admirable thing to believe: you and I are communicating with each other, making use of words, by soul towards soul.[68]

E **Alcibiades:** Definitely.

Socrates: So this is what we were talking about a little bit before: Socrates converses with Alcibiades, making use of speech—not speaking to his face, it's likely, but to Alcibiades; and this is his soul.

Alcibiades: It seems so to me.

Socrates: So he who commands that one know oneself bids us to know our souls.

131A **Alcibiades:** It seems so.

Socrates: So whoever knows any of the parts of the body knows what belongs to him, but not himself.

Alcibiades: That's so.

Socrates: So no doctor knows himself, inasmuch as he is a doctor, nor does any trainer, inasmuch as he is a trainer.

Alcibiades: It does not seem so.

Socrates: So farmers and craftsmen fall far short of knowing themselves. For they don't even know what belongs to them, it seems, but something further removed than what belongs to them, at least B as far as their arts are concerned. For they know the things that belong to the body, the things with which the body is tended.

Alcibiades: That's true.

Socrates: So if moderation[69] is knowing oneself, none of these is moderate because of his art.

Alcibiades: It does not seem so to me.

Socrates: For this reason these seem to be low-class arts and not subjects a good man need know.

---

[68] To remove any hint of using the soul, some would emend the dative *psychēi* to the accusative *psychēn* and read "you and I are communicating with words, soul to soul."

[69] The Greek *sophrosunē*, translated throughout by "moderation," literally means something like "soundmindedness." It can apply to self-control (as probably at 122c) as well as to self-knowledge.

Alcibiades: Definitely.

Socrates: So, once again, whoever tends his body tends what belongs to him and not himself.

Alcibiades: Probably.

Socrates: And whoever tends money, tends neither himself nor what C belongs to him, but something still further removed than what belongs to him?

Alcibiades: It seems so to me.

Socrates: So the moneymaker isn't doing his own work after all.

Alcibiades: Correct.

Socrates: So if someone was a lover of Alcibiades' body, it was not Alcibiades he loved, but something that belonged to Alcibiades?

Alcibiades: That's true.

Socrates: So it's he who loves your soul who loves you?

Alcibiades: That appears necessary from the argument.

Socrates: Now, the one who loves your body is going to depart, since its bloom is fading?

Alcibiades: It appears so.

D **Socrates:** But the one who loves your soul will not depart, so long as it is getting better.

Alcibiades: That's likely.

Socrates: Then I am the one who does not go off but remains as your body is fading, now that the others have departed.

Alcibiades: You've done well, Socrates—and may you not leave me.

Socrates: Well, make the effort to be as beautiful as you can be.

Alcibiades: I will make the effort.

E **Socrates:** So this is how things stand with you. There never was, it's likely, a lover of Alcibiades son of Cleinias, nor is there, save one alone—and he cherished[70]—Socrates son of Sophroniscus and Phaenarete.

---

[70] An allusion to Homer, *Odyssey* 2.364–65, where the nurse Eurycleia is attempting to persuade Telemachus not to go off searching for information about his lost father:

Why do you want to go across much country, being a lone, cherished <son>?

Alcibiades: True.

Socrates: Now you said that I had barely beat you to it in approaching you, since you would have approached me first, wanting to learn why I alone do not depart.

Alcibiades: That is how it was.

Socrates: Well, this is the reason: I alone loved you, while the others loved what belonged to you. What belongs to you is passing its prime, but you are beginning to bloom. And now, unless you are corrupted by the Athenian people and become uglier, I shall not leave you. For this is what I most fear, that you will be corrupted by becoming a people lover. Many good Athenians have already experienced this, for "the people of greathearted Erechtheus"[71] has a lovely face. But one must see them stripped. So take the precaution I'm talking about.

132A

Alcibiades: What precaution?

B **Socrates:** Exercise first, you blessed man, and learn what one must learn in order to get into the affairs of the city, and do not get into them before that, so that you may go with the countercharm in hand and not suffer anything terrible.

Alcibiades: You seem to me to have put it well, Socrates. But try to explain in what way we can take care of ourselves.

Socrates: Well, this much we've accomplished previously: we've come to a decent agreement about what we are. We were afraid that, falling short of this, we would without noticing it end up caring for something else and not for ourselves.

Alcibiades: That's so.

C **Socrates:** And after that we agreed that one must take care of the soul and look to it.

Alcibiades: Clearly.

Socrates: And taking care of bodies and of money must be handed over to others.

Alcibiades: Why, surely.

Socrates: In what way could we know these things most distinctly? Since if we know this, it's likely, we'll also know ourselves. Why—by the gods!—did we fail to understand that eloquent inscription at Delphi we mentioned just now?

---

[71] A quotation from Homer, *Iliad* 2.547, in the catalogue of ships; Erechtheus is a legendary early king of Athens.

Alcibiades: Whatever do you have in mind in saying this, Socrates?

D **Socrates:** I'll point out to you what I suspect the inscription is telling and advising us. There's probably not a parallel for it everywhere, but in the case of vision alone.

Alcibiades: What do mean by this?

Socrates: You consider it, too. If it advised our eye as if the eye were a person, saying, "See yourself," how would we understand what it was suggesting? Wouldn't it be to look at something in which the eye was going to see itself?

Alcibiades: Clearly.

E **Socrates:** Are we aware of anything in which, when we look at it, we see both it and ourselves?

Alcibiades: Clearly, Socrates, mirrors and things of that sort.

Socrates: You're correct. Now is there anything of this sort in the eye with which we see?

Alcibiades: Of course.

133A **Socrates:** So you are aware that the face of one looking at an eye appears in the pupil of the person opposite him as in a mirror; we call this the "image in the eye," as it is a reflection of the one looking at it.[72]

Alcibiades: That's true.

Socrates: So an eye beholding an eye, and looking at that which is best in it, that with which it sees, would thus see itself?

Alcibiades: It appears so.

Socrates: But if it looked at any other of the things in a person or at any other thing there is, except for that which is similar to it, it will not see itself.

B **Alcibiades:** That's true.

Socrates: So if an eye is going to see itself, it must look at an eye, and at just that place in the eye in which the excellence of the eye resides. And this, I suppose, is vision.

Alcibiades: Just so.

---

[72] The Greek word translated here as "image in the eye," *korē*, can also mean "girl," "doll," or "pupil." The image in the pupil played a central role in many ancient theories of vision.

Socrates: So, my friend Alcibiades, if a soul is to know itself, it must look into a soul, and particularly into that region of it in which the excellence of the soul, wisdom, resides, and to anything else that this is similar to?

Alcibiades: It seems so to me, Socrates.

C **Socrates:** Can we say that anything in the soul is more divine than that which is concerned with knowing and thought?

Alcibiades: We cannot.

Socrates: So it is to God[73] that this aspect of soul is similar, and one looking to this and knowing all that is divine, both God and thought, would in this way also most know himself.

Alcibiades: It appears so.

<**Socrates:** Then just as mirrors are clearer than the reflector in the eye and purer and more brilliant, so also God is more pure and more brilliant than that which is best in our soul?

Alcibiades: That's likely, Socrates.

Socrates: So looking to God we would make use of the most beautiful reflector and, among human things, looking to the excellence of the soul, and in this way we would best see and know ourselves.

Alcibiades: Yes.>[74]

Socrates: And we agreed that knowing oneself is moderation.[75]

Alcibiades: Of course.

---

[73] The Greeks sometimes used the singular for god, *theos*, in contexts that show that neither "the god" or "a god" is meant, leaving us with "God." But no commitment to monotheism is implied; rather *theos* stands in for the qualities the gods share as gods, and often approaches "the gods" in meaning. Here some manuscripts read *toi theioi*, "the divine," in place of the text I render as "God," *toi theoi*; the meaning is not greatly changed either way.

[74] These lines, like those at 115e and 128a above, are not found in manuscripts of the *Alcibiades I*, but only in quotations from later authors. Some (e.g., Denyer 2001: 236–237) argue that this passage has linguistic oddities and is a Christian or Neoplatonic interpolation. Others (e.g., Johnson 1999: 11–14) argue that an apparent cross-reference to it at 134d shows that it is authentic (and the later passage is in the manuscript tradition, so there is no independent reason for deleting it).

[75] Compare 131b.

Socrates: Then if we do not know ourselves, and are not moderate, could we know the things that belong to us, both good and bad?

Alcibiades: How could that happen, Socrates?

D **Socrates:** For perhaps it appears to you impossible for one who does not know Alcibiades to recognize that the things that belong to Alcibiades do belong to Alcibiades.

Alcibiades: Impossible indeed, by Zeus.

Socrates: Nor is it possible for us to know that our things are ours, if we do not know ourselves.

Alcibiades: How could that be?

Socrates: And if we do not know our things, we cannot know what belongs to our things either?

Alcibiades: It does not appear so.

Socrates: So we were not altogether correct to agree just now[76] that there are some who do not know themselves, but know what belongs to them, and others who only know what belongs to their belongings. For it seems that it is a matter for one person and one art to know E all of these things: oneself, what belongs to one, and what belongs to one's belongings.

Alcibiades: Probably.

Socrates: And he who is ignorant about what belongs to him is also, I suppose, ignorant of what belongs to others in the same way.

Alcibiades: Why, surely.

Socrates: Now, if he is ignorant about what belongs to others, he will also be ignorant about what belongs to cities?

Alcibiades: Necessarily.

Socrates: So this sort of person could not become a statesman?

Alcibiades: Certainly not.

Socrates: Nor a manager of a household.

134A **Alcibiades:** Certainly not.

Socrates: Nor will he know what he's doing.

Alcibiades: No, he won't.

Socrates: And won't he make mistakes if he doesn't know?

---

[76] 131a–c.

Alcibiades: Of course.

Socrates: And when he makes mistakes will he not do badly,[77] both in private and in public?

Alcibiades: Why, of course.

Socrates: And when he does badly won't he be wretched?

Alcibiades: Very much so.

Socrates: What about those on whose behalf he acts?

Alcibiades: They also.

Socrates: So it is not possible, unless one is moderate and good, to be happy.

B **Alcibiades:** It's not possible.

Socrates: So bad people are wretched.

Alcibiades: Very much so.

Socrates: So it's not one who's gotten rich who will avoid being wretched, but the one who has become moderate?

Alcibiades: It appears so.

Socrates: So cities do not need walls or triremes or dockyards, Alcibiades, if they are going to be happy, nor numbers or size without excellence.

Alcibiades: No indeed.

Socrates: If you are going to manage the affairs of the city correctly and C admirably, you must give excellence to the citizens.

Alcibiades: Why, of course.

Socrates: Could one give something he does not have?

Alcibiades: How could he?

Socrates: So you must first get possession of excellence yourself, as must anyone else who is going to rule and take care not only of himself and what belongs to him in private but also of the city and what belongs to it.

Alcibiades: That's true.

---

[77] "He will do badly" (*kakōs praxei*) could also be rendered "will perform badly," i.e., it may refer to unethical or unsuccessful action. Compare the ambiguity at 116b.

Socrates: So it is not authority or power to do whatever you want that you must provide for yourself or for the city, but justice and moderation.

Alcibiades: It appears so.

D **Socrates:** For by acting justly and moderately both you and the city will act in a way pleasing to God.

Alcibiades: That's likely.

Socrates: And, as we said before,[78] you both will act by looking to what is divine and brilliant.

Alcibiades: It appears so.

Socrates: Looking in that direction you will see and know both yourselves and the good things that belong to you.

Alcibiades: Yes.

Socrates: So you both will act correctly and well?

Alcibiades: Yes.

E **Socrates:** Well, if you both act like this I am willing to guarantee that both of you will indeed be happy.

Alcibiades: And you are a reliable guarantor.

Socrates: But if you act unjustly, looking to what is ungodly and dark, you will, it's likely, do ungodly and dark deeds in your ignorance of yourselves.

Alcibiades: It seems so.

Socrates: For what is likely to happen to a private individual or to 135A a city if they have the authority to do whatever they want, my friend Alcibiades, but are mindless? Take one who is sick and has the authority to do whatever he wants, but does not have the mind of a doctor, and is so tyrannical that no one checks him at all—what is going to happen to him? Isn't it likely that his body will be corrupted?

Alcibiades: That's true.

Socrates: What about on a ship, if someone has the authority to do what seems right to him, but lacks the mind and the excellence of a helmsman—do you see what would happen to him and to those on board with him?

---

[78] 133c.

Alcibiades: I do—they'd all perish.

B **Socrates:** Then in the same way, whenever a city or any office or authority lacks excellence, it follows that they will do badly?

Alcibiades: Necessarily.

Socrates: So one must not provide tyranny, my excellent Alcibiades, either for himself or for his city, if you two are to be happy, but excellence.

Alcibiades: That's true.

Socrates: And until one has excellence, it is better to be ruled by one's better than to rule—not only for a child, but for a man as well.

Alcibiades: It appears so.

Socrates: And isn't what is better also more admirable?

Alcibiades: Yes.

Socrates: And the more admirable is also more appropriate?

C **Alcibiades:** Why, of course.

Socrates: So it is appropriate for one who is bad to be a slave, since it's better.

Alcibiades: Yes.

Socrates: Then badness is appropriate for a slave.

Alcibiades: It appears so.

Socrates: And excellence appropriate for one who is free.

Alcibiades: Yes.

Socrates: Mustn't one, my companion, flee slavishness?

Alcibiades: Most of all, Socrates.

Socrates: Do you sense where you stand now? Is it appropriate for one who is free, or not?

Alcibiades: I seem to sense it all too well.

Socrates: Then do you know how you will escape from this current condition of yours? (Let's not give it its name in the case of such an admirable man.)

D **Alcibiades:** I do.

Socrates: How?

Alcibiades: If you wish it, Socrates.

Socrates: That's not admirably put, Alcibiades.

Alcibiades: How must one put it?

Socrates: If God is willing.

Alcibiades: I say it then. And in addition to this I say that we are probably going to take on new roles, Socrates, I yours and you mine. For there's no way that I'm not going to attend on you from this day forth, and you will be attended by me.

E **Socrates:** So, you noble man, my love will differ not at all from that of the stork, if having hatched a winged love in you it will in turn be tended by it.[79]

Alcibiades: Well, this is how things stand, and I will begin from this point forth to care for justice.

Socrates: I'd like you to keep on doing that. But I am filled with dread, not because I do not trust in your nature, but because I see the force of the city and fear that it will overcome both me and you.

[79] Young storks were thought to nourish their parents by feeding them with their own blood.

ALCIBIADES II

138A **Socrates:** Alcibiades, are you on your way to pray to the god?

Alcibiades: Definitely, Socrates.

Socrates: You do appear, you know, to have a dour look on your face and to be looking toward the ground, as if you were concerned about something.

Alcibiades: And what would one be concerned about, Socrates?

B **Socrates:** The greatest of concerns, Alcibiades, as it seems to me. For, by Zeus, don't you think that, whenever we pray in private or in public, the gods sometimes give us some things but not others, and that they give to some of us, but not to others?

Alcibiades: Definitely.

Socrates: Does it seem to you that there is need for much caution, in order that one not, without being aware of it, pray for the worst things, thinking them to be good, when the gods are disposed C to give whatever someone prays for? Just so, they say, Oedipus suddenly prayed that his sons would divide their inheritance with the sword.[1] When he could have asked for some relief from the bad things that he had, his curse sought other bad things in addition to the ones that were already there. So these things took place, and from them many other awful things, but what need is there to mention each?

---

[1] Oedipus' sons killed each other fighting for their inheritance, rule of Thebes. He had cursed them for their failure to take care of him in his old age. Socrates' language seems poetic, but is not a close match for any extant account of Oedipus' curse. Compare Euripides, *Phoenician Women* 66–68 (the play is certainly cited at 151b); Aeschylus, *Seven Against Thebes* 785–789; Sophocles, *Oedipus at Colonus* 1383–1392, and fragments 2 and 3 of the cyclic epic *Thebais*. In the first two Oedipus is explicitly said to be sick (Euripides) or mad-hearted (Aeschylus).

Alcibiades: But you, Socrates, are talking about a madman. For does it seem to you that anyone who was healthy would bring himself to pray for such things?

Socrates: Does being mad seem to you the opposite of being sensible?[2]

Alcibiades: Definitely.

D **Socrates:** Do some people seem to you to be foolish, and some sensible?

Alcibiades: They do indeed.

Socrates: Come on then, let's consider just who these people are. It has been agreed that there are some who are foolish and some who are sensible, and that others are mad.

Alcibiades: That has been agreed.

Socrates: Now are there some who are healthy?

Alcibiades: Some are.

Socrates: And others are unhealthy?

139A **Alcibiades:** Of course.

Socrates: And these are not the same?

Alcibiades: No, they're not.

Socrates: Now are there also some others who are in neither condition?

Alcibiades: Certainly not.

Socrates: For it's necessary, if one is a human being, either to be sick or not to be sick.

Alcibiades: It seems so to me.

Socrates: And do you have the same view of sensibleness and foolishness?

Alcibiades: What do you mean?

---

[2] *Phronein*, the word translated here and below as "sensible," can also be rendered as "prudent" or even "wise"; so also for cognates. It refers most often to the general good sense that enables one to choose what is best, as at 140e below. For Socrates on madness, compare Xenophon, *Memorabilia* 1.2.50, 3.9.6–7. On being sensible, compare *Alcibiades I* 125a–b.

Socrates: If it seems to you only possible to be either sensible or foolish—or is there some third condition in between which makes a person B neither sensible nor foolish?

Alcibiades: Certainly not.

Socrates: So it is necessary that one be in one or the other of these conditions.

Alcibiades: It seems so to me.

Socrates: Now do you remember agreeing that madness is opposite to being sensible?

Alcibiades: I do.

Socrates: And that there is no third condition in between, which makes a person neither sensible nor foolish?

Alcibiades: I did agree.

Socrates: And how indeed could two things be opposite to one?

Alcibiades: There's no way.

C **Socrates:** So foolishness and madness are probably the same thing.

Alcibiades: It appears so.

Socrates: So, Alcibiades, we would be correct to say that all who are foolish are mad. For example, some of your contemporaries, if some of them are foolish—as they are—and some of those still older than you. For, by Zeus, don't you think that few in the city are sensible, but many indeed are foolish, the ones you call mad?

Alcibiades: I do.

Socrates: Do you think, then, that we would be comfortable sharing D the city with so many madmen? Would we not, being struck and pelted and suffering all the things that madmen are in the habit of doing, have paid our penalty long ago? But look out, you blessed man: this may not be the case.

Alcibiades: So just what is the case, Socrates? For it's probably not as I thought it was.

Socrates: Nor does it seem so to me. But look at it like this.

Alcibiades: How do you mean?

Socrates: I will tell you. We do take it that some people are sick. Or don't we?

Alcibiades: We definitely do.

E **Socrates:** Now does it seem necessary to you that one who is sick has gout, or a fever, or ophthalmia, or does it seem to you that even if he has none of these conditions he may be sick with some other sickness? For there are surely many sicknesses, and not these alone.

Alcibiades: There are many of them, it seems to me.

Socrates: Now does every case of ophthalmia seem to you to be sickness?

Alcibiades: Yes.

Socrates: Then is every case of sickness ophthalmia?

Alcibiades: It certainly doesn't seem so to me. Yet I'm at a loss about what I should say.

140A **Socrates:** Well, if you put your mind to it with me, searching two together[3] we will perhaps discover it.

Alcibiades: Well, I am putting my mind to it, Socrates, to the best of my ability.

Socrates: Now was it agreed by us that all ophthalmia is sickness, yet all sickness is not ophthalmia.

Alcibiades: It was agreed.

Socrates: And it does seem to me that our agreement was correct. For those with a fever are all sick, yet not all who are sick have a B fever, or gout, or ophthalmia, I think. All of these sorts of things are sicknesses, but those we call doctors say that their symptoms differ. For they are not alike in all cases, nor do they have similar effects, but each has its own capacity. Yet they are all sicknesses. In the same way we take some people to be craftsmen. Or don't we?

Alcibiades: Definitely.

Socrates: There are cobblers and carpenters and sculptors and a whole host of others, but what need is there to mention each? They all

---

[3] Socrates adapts *Iliad* 10.224-6, the Greek equivalent of "two heads are better than one":

> *Going two together, one of them will notice first*
> *what brings advantage; one by himself, even should he be thoughtful,*
> *still there is less intelligence to him, and his cunning has less weight.*

Diomedes has just volunteered to go on a dangerous scouting mission, but hopes to have a companion, who will turn out to be Odysseus. The same line is used at *Symposium* 174d and *Protagoras* 348d.

C possess a part of craftsmanship, which they've divided up, and all of them are craftsmen, yet not all who are craftsmen are carpenters, or cobblers, or sculptors.

Alcibiades: Certainly not.

Socrates: Well, in the same way people have divided up foolishness, and we call those who have the greatest share of it madmen, those who have a little less, silly and stupid. Some of those wanting to use euphemisms say that they are "above it all,"[4] others call them naïve, while still others call them innocents or inexperienced or D dumb. You'll find many other terms, if you look for them. All these are foolishness, but differ, just as art appeared to us different from art, and sickness from sickness. Or how does it seem to you?

Alcibiades: That's how it seems to me.

Socrates: Let's return to the beginning again from this point. For surely at the beginning of the discussion we also had to consider just who the foolish and the sensible are, since it was agreed that there are some of both. Wasn't it?

Alcibiades: Yes, it was agreed.

E **Socrates:** Now do you take the sensible to be those who know what should be done and what should be said?

Alcibiades: I do.

Socrates: Which are the foolish? Those knowing neither of these things?

Alcibiades: Yes, those.

Socrates: Now those who know neither of these things will, without being aware of it, both say and do what shouldn't be said or done?

Alcibiades: It appears so.

141A **Socrates:** Well, I was saying, Alcibiades, that Oedipus was one of these people. You will still find many people today who are not in a rage, as he was, and do not think that they are praying for bad things for themselves, but good. He didn't think so, or pray so, but there are others who are in the opposite condition. Here's what I think you'd do, first of all. Suppose the god you are on your way to pray to appeared and asked, before you had prayed for

[4] *Megalopsychos*, which more literally means "great-souled," usually refers to nobility, generosity, or arrogance; it is used of Alcibiades himself at 150c.

anything, if it would suffice for you to become tyrant of the city of Athens. If you were to believe that this was something of no account and nothing big, he would add tyranny over all the Greeks, B and if he were to see that this still seemed too little to you, unless all of Europe were added, he would promise this too, and not only this, but he would promise that, as you want, all men would perceive at once that Alcibiades son of Cleinias was tyrant. I think that you yourself would go off very pleased, thinking that you had hit upon the greatest of goods.[5]

Alcibiades: I think, Socrates, that anyone else would also, if such things happened to him.

C **Socrates:** But yet you wouldn't give your life[6] for the land of, and tyranny over, all the Greeks and barbarians?

Alcibiades: I don't think so. For how could I, if I wasn't going to be able to make any use of them?

Socrates: What if you were going to make bad and harmful use of them? You wouldn't want them like that, would you?

Alcibiades: Certainly not.

Socrates: So you see that it is unsafe either to simply accept whatever D is given or to pray oneself that it happen, at least if one is going to be harmed through this, or absolutely lose one's life. We could speak of many who have desired tyranny before now and striven to gain it for themselves, thinking that they would accomplish something good, and, because they plotted tyranny, had their lives taken away. I think that you have heard about some things that took place "yesterday or the day before," when Archelaus the tyrant of Macedon was killed by his boyfriend, who loved tyranny no less than Archelaus loved him, and thought that he E would become tyrant and a happy man.[7] But he, after holding the tyranny for three or four days, was himself plotted against by some others, and met his end.

---

[5] For Alcibiades' ambitions and the god's epiphany, compare *Alcibiades I* 105a–c.

[6] Greek *psyche*, elsewhere translated as "soul."

[7] The quotation is from *Iliad* 2.303, where Odysseus vividly remembers, as if it were the day before yesterday, when the Greeks were marshalling against Troy nine years ago and the seer Chalcas predicted their success after nine years. Archelaus murdered the legitimate king of Macedonia in 413 and ruled until he was murdered in 399. He had attracted to his court leading Athenian poets, including Agathon and Euripides; Socrates, we are told, refused a similar invitation (Aristotle, *Rhetoric* 1398a24). Compare *Gorgias* 470d–471d.

You also see that some of our own fellow citizens—and this we haven't merely heard from others, but know ourselves at first A hand—desired to become general and achieved this, but some of them are even now still in exile from this city, while others have ended their lives. Those who are thought to have done the best came through many dangers and fears, not only while serving as general, but when they came back to their own home, besieged as they were by informers in no less a siege than that they endured at the hands of the enemy.[8] The result is that some of them would pray to never have been general rather than to have served as B general. Now if the dangers and labors led to some benefit, it would make sense. But, as it is, it is quite the opposite.

You will find that it is the same way concerning children, that some who prayed before now to have them, had them, only to fall into misfortunes and griefs of the greatest sort. Some of them had children who were completely bad, and spent their whole C lives in grief. Others' children were good, but met with misfortune which took them from their parents, who thus met with no less ill fortune than the others and would wish that their children had never been born.

But even though these things and many others like them are so very clear, it is rare to find anyone who would refuse what is given, or, if he were going to get something through prayer, would stop praying. The many[9] would not refuse tyranny, were it given to D them, or the generalship, or many other things that, when present, do more harm than benefit: they would even pray to get them, if they don't have them already. A little while later they sometimes change their tune, unpraying the things they had prayed for at first. I can find no way to deny that it is truly vain for men to blame the gods by claiming that bad things come to them from the gods. "But they themselves by their own recklessness"—or foolishness, whichever we should call it— "have pains beyond what is fated."[10]

---

[8] Generals were the highest elected officials in Athens, and like all public officials were subject to scrutiny at the end of their terms.

[9] Greek *hoi polloi*, which is sometimes rendered in the *Alcibiades II* by "most people": see the note at *Alcibiades I*, 110e.

[10] Socrates adapts Zeus' words at Homer, *Odyssey* 1.32–34:

> *Ah, how mortals blame the gods in vain.*
> *For they say that evils come from us. But they themselves*
> *through their own recklessness have pains beyond what is fated.*

Zeus goes on to note that Aegisthus, who seduced Agamemnon's wife, killed Agamemnon upon his return home from Troy, and then was killed by Agamemnon's son, Orestes, had been warned by the gods and thus had nothing to complain about.

E He was probably sensible, Alcibiades, the poet who, it seems to me, was dealing with some mindless friends. He saw that they were doing and praying for things that weren't for the best, but seemed to them to be, and he made this prayer on behalf of all of them in common. He says something like this:

143A *King Zeus, good things, whether we pray for them or not give us, and ward off foul things even when we pray for them.*[11]

So he bids. To me the poet seems to speak both admirably and safely. If you have anything in mind about this, don't keep silent.

Alcibiades: It is difficult, Socrates, to speak against things that have been admirably said. Now I'm aware of how many bad things B ignorance causes for people, whenever it's the likely reason that we aren't aware that we are doing and, to top it all, praying for, the worst of things for ourselves. Nobody would think this is so, since everyone thinks that he is up to this, to pray for what is best for himself, and not what is worst. For that truly would be like a curse, not a prayer.

Socrates: But perhaps, best of men, a man who is wiser than you and I would say that we aren't speaking correctly in simply blaming C ignorance, at least if we do not add that ignorance of some things, and for some people, and for people in a certain state, is good, as it is bad for others.

Alcibiades: What do you mean? Is there anything that anyone in any state is better off not knowing than knowing?

Socrates: It seems so to me. But not to you?

Alcibiades: No indeed, by Zeus.

Socrates: Well, I will not charge you with wanting to do to your mother what Orestes did, they say, and Alcmaeon, and if there are any D others who did the same as they.[12]

Alcibiades: By Zeus, Socrates, hush!

Socrates: You shouldn't, Alcibiades, tell one to hush who says that you wouldn't be willing to do these things, but far more anyone who said the opposite, since this seems to you to be such a fearful thing that one must not even speak of it in this way. But do you think

---

[11] The original poet is unknown, and the wording and even the precise extent of the quotation are uncertain, though its gist is clear enough. A version of the poem is included as 10.108 in the *Palatine Anthology*. For Socrates' prayers, compare Xenophon, *Memorabilia* 1.3.2.

[12] In myth both Orestes and Alcmaeon killed their mothers for killing, or at least helping to kill, their fathers.

that Orestes, if he were sensible and knew what was best for him to do, would have brought himself to do any of these things?

Alcibiades: Certainly not.

E **Socrates:** Nor, I think, anyone else.

Alcibiades: No indeed.

Socrates: Ignorance of what is best is a bad thing, then, it's likely, as is not knowing what is best.

Alcibiades: To me it seems so.

Socrates: Does it also seem bad both for that person himself, and for everyone else?

Alcibiades: I say so.

Socrates: Now let's consider this case also. What if it suddenly occurred to you, because you thought it was better, to take a dagger and go to the house of your own guardian and friend, Pericles,[13] and ask if he were inside, wanting to kill him, and no one else, and they should say that he was inside. I'm not saying that you want to do any of these things. But what if, I'm thinking, this did seem best to you—and surely nothing stops one who does not know what is best from believing that the worst of things is the best. Or doesn't that seem so to you?

144A

Alcibiades: Definitely.

B **Socrates:** Well, if you were to go inside and see that very man, but did not know that it was he and thought he was someone else, would you still bring yourself to kill him?

Alcibiades: No, by Zeus, it doesn't seem so to me.

Socrates: For, surely, it wasn't just anyone you met, but that very man whom you wanted. Wasn't it?

Alcibiades: Yes.

Socrates: Now if you were to try many times, but always, whenever you were going to do this, did not know that it was Pericles, you would never attack him.

Alcibiades: Certainly not.

---

[13] Pericles was Athens' most influential politician at the dramatic date of this conversation. On Pericles and his relationship to Alcibiades, see *Alcibiades I* 104b (and the note on that passage) and Section 2 of the Introduction.

Socrates: And does it seem to you that Orestes would have attacked his mother, if, in the same way, he didn't know that it was her?

C **Alcibiades:** I for my part don't think so.

Socrates: For it surely wasn't just any woman he met that he intended to kill, nor anyone's mother, but to kill his own mother himself.

Alcibiades: That's so.

Socrates: So for people who are in this sort of state and have this sort of belief it is better not to know this sort of thing.

Alcibiades: It appears so.

Socrates: You see, then, that ignorance of some things, and for some people, and for people in a certain state, is good, and not bad, as it had seemed to you just now.

Alcibiades: That's likely.

D **Socrates:** Now if you want to consider the next thing, it may perhaps seem strange to you.

Alcibiades: Just what is that, Socrates?

Socrates: Practically speaking, the possession of any other knowledge, if one does not possess knowledge of what is best, rarely benefits, and most often harms the one who has it. Consider it like this. Doesn't it seem necessary to you that, whenever we are going to either do or say something, we must first either believe that we E know or really know whatever we are so ready to say or do?

Alcibiades: It seems so to me.

Socrates: So the speakers in the Assembly, for example, will give us advice either knowing how to do so or believing that they do—some speaking about war and peace, some about the construction 145A of walls or the maintenance of harbors. And, in a word, whatever the city does regarding another city or itself by itself is all done on the advice given by these speakers.

Alcibiades: That's true.

Socrates: Well, look at what follows from this.

Alcibiades: If I can.

Socrates: You surely call some sensible and some foolish.

Alcibiades: I do.

Socrates: And you call most people foolish, and few sensible.

Alcibiades: Just so.

Socrates: And in both cases you are looking to something?

Alcibiades: Yes.

B **Socrates:** So do you call someone sensible if he knows how to give advice, but does not know whether it is better to do so, or when it is better to do so?[14]

Alcibiades: Certainly not.

Socrates: Nor, I think, do you call anyone sensible who knows how to wage war, but doesn't know when it is better, and for how long it is better. Isn't that so?

Alcibiades: Yes.

Socrates: Nor, then, if someone knows how to kill someone, or deprive him of his money and exile him from his country, but not whether it was better to do this, and to whom it was better to do this?

Alcibiades: No indeed.

C **Socrates:** So whoever knows something of this sort, if knowledge of what is best accompanies him—and this, surely, is the same as the knowledge of what is beneficial, isn't it?

Alcibiades: Yes.

Socrates: It's he that we will say is sensible and a sufficient adviser both for the city and for himself. Of one who isn't this sort we'll say the opposite of this. Or how does it seem to you?

Alcibiades: That's how it seems to me.

Socrates: And what if someone knows how to ride a horse or shoot a bow, or how to box or wrestle or perform in any other contest, D or do anything else of the sort of things we know by means of art—what will you call whoever knows what turns out better when it is done according to a given art? Isn't he who knows what's done better according to horsemanship a horseman?

Alcibiades: I think so.

Socrates: And for boxing it's a boxer, and for aulos playing it's an aulos player,[15] and the rest, I suppose, analogously to this. Or does it somehow work differently?

Alcibiades: No, that's how it is.

---

[14] For a similar discussion of what is better, see *Alcibiades I* 107d–108e.

[15] On the aulos, see the note at *Alcibiades I* 106e.

Socrates: Now does it seem necessary to you that one who is E knowledgeable about one of these things is a sensible man, or will we say that he's far from it?

Alcibiades: He's far from it, by Zeus.

Socrates: So what sort of community do you think would consist of good archers and aulos players, and good athletes and other artists as well, and mixed in with these the ones we were just talking about, those who know only how to wage war and how to kill, and also men who are public speakers full of political hot air, if all of these are without the knowledge of what is best and without the one 146A who knows when and on whom it is better to make use of each one of these arts?

Alcibiades: I think it would be a poor excuse for a community, Socrates.

Socrates: You would say so, I think, when you saw each one of them vying for honor in and distributing the greatest share in the community

to this
where he himself is at his best.[16]

I mean that which comes out best when done according to the given art. But he errs for the most part regarding what is best for the city and for himself, because, I think, he has put his trust in B opinion rather than intelligence. This being the case, would we not be correct to say that this sort of community would be full of great confusion and disorder?

Alcibiades: Correct indeed, by Zeus.

Socrates: Now does it seem to us that we must first think that we know or really know whatever we are ready to do or say?

Alcibiades: It does seem so.

Socrates: And if someone does something he knows, or thinks he knows, C and "beneficially" is added, we must consider him profitable both to the city and to himself?

Alcibiades: Why, of course.

Socrates: And, I think, if it's the opposite of this, neither to the city nor to himself.

Alcibiades: Certainly not.

---

[16] At *Gorgias* 485e, Plato has Callicles paraphrase and quote this fragment from Euripides' *Antiope* at greater length: "Each man is brilliant in this, and hastens after this,

attributing the greatest share of the day to this
where he himself is at his best."

Socrates: And does it still seem to you the same way, or is it different somehow?

Alcibiades: No, it's like this.

Socrates: Now did you say that you called most people foolish, and few sensible?

Alcibiades: I did.

Socrates: And we say again that the many are mistaken about what is best, since, I think, they trust in opinion rather than intelligence.

D **Alcibiades:** We do say so.

Socrates: So it is profitable for most people neither to know nor to think that they know, if, that is, they are more eager to do the things they know or think they know, and in so doing will be harmed most of the time rather than benefited.

Alcibiades: That is very true.

Socrates: You do see, then, that I was in reality obviously correct to say E that the possession of other knowledge, if someone possesses it without knowledge of the best, is probably rarely beneficial and most often harmful to the one who has it?

Alcibiades: Even if it didn't seem so then, it does seem so now, Socrates.

Socrates: So if either a city or a soul is going to live correctly it must get hold of this knowledge, just as one who is sick must get hold 147A of a doctor, and one who is going to sail safely a helmsman. For without this, the more brilliantly the fair wind of fortune blows for gaining property, bodily vigor, or anything else of this sort, the more errors necessarily come to pass from such things. He who has what it takes to be called a polymath and a jack of all trades, but is bereft of this knowledge of the best and is led about by each one of these other sorts of knowledge, won't he really experience B a great storm, and justly too, since, I think, he continues on the ocean without a helmsman, cruising for no long lifetime? The result here too, it seems to me, is the one the poet describes, making an accusation against someone, I suppose, that "many things he knew, but badly he knew all of them."[17]

---

[17] This paraphrase is one of our few pieces of evidence for the *Margites*, a mock-epic sometimes attributed to Homer that detailed the various misadventures of its idiotic title character. Socrates' interpretation of it below is every bit as forced as his interpretation of Simonides at *Protagoras* 339a–348c.

Alcibiades: And just how is the saying of the poet fitting, Socrates? For it doesn't seem to me to be at all relevant.

Socrates: It's very relevant indeed. But, best of men, he speaks enigmatically, both he and nearly all poets. For all of poetry is by nature enigmatic and not a matter for just any man to understand. C Given its nature, whenever it takes hold of a man who is envious and does not want to reveal his wisdom but to hide it as much as possible, understanding just what each poet has in mind is clearly supernaturally difficult. For you don't think, surely, that Homer, the most godlike and wisest of the poets, did not recognize that it is impossible to know badly—for it's he who says that Margites D knows many things, but knows all of them badly. But he made a riddle, I think, using "badly" in place of "bad," and "he knew" in place of "to know." Put together, then, it becomes this (not in the original meter, but this is what he wanted to say): "he knew many things, but it was bad for him to know all of them." It's clear, then, that if it was bad for him to know many things, he didn't amount to much, at least if one should trust what has been said previously.

E **Alcibiades:** Well, that's the way it seems to me, Socrates. Indeed, I would find it difficult to trust in anything else that's said, if not in that.

Socrates: And the way it seems to you is correct.

Alcibiades: Then again, it seems otherwise to me.

Socrates: But, come, by Zeus! For you see, surely, what it means to be this lost, and you seem to me to share in being lost yourself. You change back and forth, you know, and don't stop anywhere, but however it may seem to you, you toss it aside again and it no 148A longer seems that way to you. What if, even now, the god you are on the way to pray to were to appear, before you had prayed for anything, and ask if one of those things that were spoken of at the beginning will suffice for you, or if he were to leave it to you to pray for yourself? Just how do you think that you would, by accepting something given by him or praying for something yourself, hit upon what was called for?[18]

Alcibiades: Well, by the gods, I don't have anything to say to you offhand, Socrates. This seems to me to be something as ludicrous B as Margites, and truly calling for much caution: how not to pray, without being aware of it, for what is bad, when it seems to be

---

[18] For Socrates' rebuke of Alcibiades, compare *Alcibiades I* 113e; for Alcibiades' vacillation, compare *Alcibiades I* 116e-117a; for the imagined divine epiphany, compare *Alcibiades I* 105a.

good, and then a little later, as you were saying, sing a different tune, unpraying whatever was prayed for at first.

Socrates: Then doesn't that poet know something more than us, the one I mentioned at the beginning of our discussion, who bid the gods to ward off foul things even when we prayed for them?

Alcibiades: It seems so to me.

C **Socrates:** Well, Alcibiades, the Lacedaemonians also esteemed this man, or observed this for themselves, and in both private and public they always make a very similar prayer, bidding the gods to give them admirable things in addition to good ones. No one ever hears them pray for more than that. This is why up to this point in time they have been no less fortunate than any other people. If, after all, they too have not been fortunate in all things, this is not D because of their prayer, but it is up to the gods, I think, either to give whatever someone prays for or the opposite of that.

I want to recount something else, which I once heard from some old men. The Athenians and Lacedaemonians were at odds, and whenever a battle took place our city always met with misfortune both by land and by sea and was never able to get the E upper hand. So the Athenians, troubled by this and at a loss to find out what means they must use to turn aside the bad things they were suffering, took counsel and decided that it was best to send to Ammon[19] and ask him. Now in addition to asking that, they asked him just why it was that the gods gave victory to the Lacedaemonians rather than to them. "We," they said, "give more numerous and more admirable sacrifices than the rest of the Greeks; we adorn the sanctuaries of the gods with offerings as no others do; we give the gods the most expensive and most 149A august processions each year; and we spend more than all the other Greeks combined. But the Lacedaemonians," they said, "have never been concerned with any of this, and care so little for the gods that they are always sacrificing maimed animals and honor the gods in every way no little bit less fittingly than we do, though they possess no less wealth than our city does." When they had said this, they asked what they should do to find release from the B bad things they were suffering. The priest who speaks for the god made no other answer than this—for clearly the god would not allow it—but called them and said, "To the Athenians Ammon

[19] Ammon, the chief god of the Egyptian pantheon, was identified with Zeus by the Greeks.

says this. He declares that he would prefer the reverent Laconic speech[20] to all the sacrifices of the Greeks put together." This much he said, and no more.

Now by this "reverent speech" it seems to me that the god meant nothing else than their prayer. For, in reality, it is far superior to the prayers of others. The rest of the Greeks, those who (C) have brought out cows with gilded horns, and the others who give the gods offerings, pray for whatever it happens to be, whether good or bad. Hearing their irreverent speech, then, the gods do not accept their expensive processions and sacrifices. Rather, it seems to me that there is need of much caution and consideration as to just what is to be said and what not.

(D) You'll also find very similar things said in Homer. He says that the Trojans, when they were making their bivouac

Sacrificed complete hecatombs to the immortals.

And the winds bore the smell of the sacrifice from the plain to the sky

sweet it was; but the blessed gods took no part of it,
nor wished to; for sacred Troy was hateful to them
and Priam and the people of Priam of the stout ash spear.[21]

(E) So it did them no good to sacrifice and give gifts in vain, hated as they were by the gods. For the gods, I think, are not of the sort to be turned by gifts, like some bad moneylender. Rather, we are saying something naïve in deeming the Lacedaemonians worthy because they excel in this. For it would be an awful thing if the gods looked to our gifts and sacrifices and not to our souls, to see (150A) whether we are pious and just. They look to this, I think, far more than to these expensive processions and sacrifices; nothing stops either an individual or a city that has done many wrongs to the gods, and many to men, from performing these every year. But the gods, as they do not take bribes, despise all of these things, as the god and the priest who speaks for him say. For both among gods and among intelligent men both justice and being sensible

---

[20] The Greek for "reverent speech" is *euphēmia*; forms of it are translated by "euphemisms" at 140c and "hush" at 143d.

[21] The lines related in meter (indented above) are found in no manuscript of the *Iliad* and are rejected by modern editors. The line partially quoted and partially paraphrased in between the lines of verse, *Iliad* 8.549, is in our manuscript text. The verses could reflect an alternative oral tradition of Homer, but, given their aptness here, are more likely a deliberate misquotation. The Trojans, in Achilles' absence, had managed to push the Greeks back and camp out on the plains of Troy; but they would, of course, eventually be pushed back and defeated.

B are probably surpassingly honored. And the sensible and the just are no others than those who know what one should do and say both to gods and to men. But I'd like to hear whatever it is that you think about this.

Alcibiades: Well, Socrates, it seems to me no different than it seems to you and to the god. For it wouldn't be proper for me to vote against the god.

Socrates: Do you remember saying that you were absolutely lost about C how to avoid praying, without being aware of it, for bad things that seemed to be good?

Alcibiades: I do.

Socrates: You see, then, that it is not safe for you to go to the god to pray to him. He could hear you speaking irreverently and accept nothing from your sacrifice—and it's possible that it could turn out even worse for you. So to me it seems best that you keep quiet. Because you are "above it all" (this is the most beautiful of the terms for foolishness), I don't think you'd be willing to use the prayer of the D Lacedaemonians. So it is necessary to wait until one learns what stance one should take toward gods and toward men.

Alcibiades: So when will this time be at hand, Socrates, and who is going to educate me? I think I'd be delighted to see just who that person is.

Socrates: He's the one concerned about you. But it seems to me, just as Homer says that Athena removed the mist from the eyes of Diomedes,

so he might well recognize both god and man alike.[22]

E so too it is necessary that one remove the mist from your soul, the mist that is there now, and only then apply that through which you are going to recognize both bad and good alike. You don't seem to me to be able to do this now.

Alcibiades: Let him take away the mist, or anything else, if he wants to. For I am prepared to flee from none of his commands, whoever the person is, at least if it will make me better.

151A **Socrates:** And it is indeed amazing how much eagerness he has on your behalf.

---

[22] *Iliad* 5.128, put into the past tense. Athena restores the wounded Greek Diomedes, in the midst of his great run against the Trojans, removes the mist that prevents him from telling immortals from mortals, and tells him he should shun battle with the gods, except for Aphrodite.

Alcibiades: Well, it seems best to me to put off the sacrifice until that time.

Socrates: You're correct. For it is more safe than to run so great a risk.

B **Alcibiades:** But what's next, Socrates? Well, since you seem to me to have given me admirable advice, I'll crown you with this wreath.[23] We'll give the gods both wreaths and the other customary things when I see that day coming. It will come before long, if the gods are willing.

Socrates: Well, I accept this, and I'd gladly see myself accepting anything else given by you. It's just like what Euripides has Creon say, when he sees Teiresias wearing wreaths and hears that he has taken the first fruits from the enemy through his art:

I hold your victorious wreaths to be an omen,
C *for we are in stormy seas, as you know yourself.*[24]

Just so, I hold this opinion of yours to be an omen. It seems to me that I am in no less stormy seas than Creon, and I would like to be victorious over your lovers.

---

[23] Compare *Symposium* 213e.

[24] Euripides, *Phoenician Women* 858–859. As Teiresias returns to Thebes after helping the Athenians to a victory, Creon asks him how Thebes can fight off the attack of the Seven Against Thebes, the army led by Polyneices, son of Oedipus, whose brother Eteocles had refused to share rule with him as they had agreed. Teiresias reveals that Creon must sacrifice his son Menoeceus if Thebes is to defeat the attackers; he refuses to do so, but Menoeceus kills himself to save the city. See the discussion at the end of Section 5 of the Introduction.

ALCIBIADES' SPEECH FROM PLATO'S *SYMPOSIUM* (212C–223B)

Our passage comes from the end of Apollodorus' account of a famous dinner party at Agathon's house in 416 B.C.; Apollodorus was not at the party himself but had learned of it from Aristodemus, who was there. Agathon had won the prize for tragedy the day before the party. Others present at the party included Pausanias, Agathon's lover; Aristophanes, the comic poet who had ridiculed Socrates in his Clouds; *Phaedrus, the man who suggested that the group praise Love* (eros); *the stuffy doctor Eryximachus; and Socrates himself. All had spoken in praise of Love, concluding with Socrates, who couched his speech as an account of what he had learned about love from a wise woman from Mantineia, Diotima, who is otherwise unknown. For more on Alcibiades' speech as a reaction to that of Socrates, see the Introduction, section 1.*

212C The others praised what Socrates had said, but Aristophanes was trying to say something, because Socrates had called him to mind by speaking about his speech.[1] Suddenly knocking on the outer door produced a great racket, like that of people partying, and they heard the voice of an aulos girl.[2] "Boys,"[3] said Agathon, "aren't you going to go see what D this is? If it is someone I know, let him in. Otherwise, say that we're not drinking anymore but have already stopped."

It wasn't long before they heard the voice of Alcibiades in the courtyard. He was very drunk and shouting at the top of his voice, asking where Agathon was and demanding that he be led to Agathon.

---

[1] At 205d–206a Socrates had "remembered" how Diotima had refuted the notion that love was for one's missing half, which had been the moral of Aristophanes' speech at 189c–195a.

[2] Slave girls who played the aulos (a sort of oboe: see the note at *Alcibiades I* 106e) were also cheap prostitutes. An aulos girl had been banished from the party at 176e to make way for a sober discussion of love.

[3] Thus one addressed slaves of whatever age.

So they led him in to them, the aulos girl supporting him with the help E of some of the others in his retinue. He stood at the door, crowned with a crown of ivy and violets and with a great many garlands on his head.[4] "Gentlemen, greetings," he said. "Will you allow a man who is really very drunk to drink with you, or should we leave after we've put these on Agathon, which is why we've come? Yesterday, you know, I couldn't be here, but now I've come to put these garlands on his head, the head, I do declare, of a most wise and most beautiful man. Are you 213A laughing at me because I'm drunk? Even if you do laugh, I know well that what I'm saying is true. Just tell me right away, am I to enter on these terms, or not? Will you drink with me, or not?"

Now everyone shouted their approval and told him to come in and lie down,[5] and Agathon called him over. He came in led by some of his people, at the same time taking off the garlands to put them on Agathon. Since he held them in front of his eyes, he didn't see Socrates, and he B sat down beside Agathon and in between him and Socrates, as Socrates had moved over when he saw him. Once he'd sat down beside Agathon, he embraced him and put the garlands on him.

Then Agathon said, "Take off his sandals, boys, so he can be our third."

"Of course," said Alcibiades. "But who's this third man drinking with us?" And as soon as he turned around he saw Socrates, and at that sight he jumped up and said, "Heracles, what's this? Is this *Socrates*? You were C lying in wait for me here again, just as you are in the habit of suddenly appearing wherever I least expect you! Why did you come here now? And why are you lying here? You're not at the side of Aristophanes or anyone one else who is laughable (and wants to be) but you've figured out a way to lie down beside the most beautiful of those here."

Now Socrates said, "Look, Agathon, are you going to defend me? For my love for this man is no light matter. From the very time when D I fell in love with him, I've never been able to look at or talk with

---

[4] Revelers were often depicted wearing such crowns of ivy, as was Dionysus, the god of drinking (and drama). Crowns of violets were associated with Aphrodite, the Muses, and Athens. The garlands were bands or ribbons worn around the head, often by victors.

[5] The Greeks dined and drank reclining diagonally on couches, propped on their left arms, with their heads toward tables in the center of the room from which they took their food and drink. Normally two reclined on a single couch, but Agathon's couch is apparently large enough for three: Agathon, Alcibiades, and Socrates from left to right (or top to bottom).

anyone who's beautiful, or this one so envies and begrudges me that it's amazing what he does and how he abuses me. He can hardly keep himself from laying hands on me. See to it that he doesn't do this now, but reconcile us, or, if he attempts to use force, defend me, as I am full of dread at his madness and his affection toward the man who loves him."

"But there's no reconciling me and you," said Alcibiades. "Well, E I will get my revenge on you for this some other time. Now give me some of the garlands, Agathon," he said, "to put on this man's amazing head, so he doesn't blame me because I put them on you, but didn't do it for him, when he is victorious over all men in words, not just the other day, as you were, but always." And at once he took some of the garlands, put them on Socrates, and lay down.[6]

Once he had lain down, he said, "All right, gentlemen. You seem to me all too sober. Now it's not to be left up to you, for we're to drink. That's what we agreed. My choice for master of ceremonies, until you've had enough to drink, is myself. Well, Agathon, if there's some big cup, have it brought out. No, there's no need. Boy, just bring us that jug."[7] 214A He had seen one which held about a half gallon. He filled it, drank it down himself, then told them to fill it for Socrates and said, "In Socrates' case, gentlemen, this wise move of mine will do me no good. For however much anyone tells him to drink, he drinks it down and is no more drunk than ever."

Now a boy filled the jug and Socrates drank it. "What sort of B drinking is this, Alcibiades?" said Eryximachus. "Is there going to be no conversation, just like this, and no song with our wine, but we're drinking just like we're parched?"

Then Alcibiades said, "Eryximachus, best of men, son of the best and most temperate father, greetings."

"You too," said Eryximachus. "But what are we going to do?"

"Whatever you tell us. For you must be obeyed—

As a doctor in battle is many men worth[8]

So command us as you see fit."

---

6 For Alcibiades putting garlands on Socrates, compare *Alcibiades II*, 151b.

7 Alcibiades chooses a *psykter*, the cooling vessel in which wine was held before it was mixed with water, in place of the shallow saucer-shaped cups the Greeks usually drank out of in an effort to moderate their intake of wine.

8 *Iliad* 11.514. Nestor asks Idomeneus to get the wounded doctor Machaon to safety.

"Listen, then," said Eryximachus. "Before you came we had decided that each of us in turn from left to right should give the most admirable[9] C speech he could about Love, and praise him. The rest of us have spoken. Since you've not spoken but have drunk, it's only just that you speak, and, once you've spoken, command Socrates to do whatever you want, and he'll do the same for the one on his right, and so on."

"Well," said Alcibiades, "that's admirably said, Eryximachus, but it may not be fair to compare a drunken man with the words of sober ones. And, you blessed man, does Socrates convince you of anything D he said? Or do you know that everything is the opposite of what he was saying? For this man, if I praise anyone in his presence, any god or man other than him, he won't keep his hands off me."

"Won't you hush?" said Socrates.

"No, by Poseidon," said Alcibiades. "You've got nothing to say about it, as I couldn't praise anyone else in your presence."

"Well, do so, if you wish," said Eryximachus, "praise Socrates."

E "What do you mean?" said Alcibiades. "Has it been decided that that's what I must do, Eryximachus? Am I to have at the man and get my revenge in front of you all?"

"Hey!" said Socrates, "what do you intend to do? Are you praising me for laughs? Or what are you going to do?"

"I will speak the truth. Let's see if you'll allow me to."

"But of course," he said, "so long as it's the truth, I allow you and bid you to tell it."

"I can't do it soon enough," said Alcibiades. "And here's what you should do. If I say something that isn't true, interrupt me at once, if you want to, and say that I'm saying something false. For I'll say nothing 215A false on purpose. If I remember things out of order, don't wonder: it's not easy for a man in my condition to give a fluent and orderly account of how strange you are.

"I will attempt to praise Socrates, gentlemen, through likenesses. Now he will perhaps think that this is for laughs, but my image will be for the sake of truth, not laughter. I say that he is very like those B silens[10] you see sitting in the statue shops, the ones the craftsmen

---

[9] Or most beautiful, the superlative of *kalos*. Forms of *kalos* are regularly translated by "beautiful" or "admirable." See the note at *Alcibiades I* 108c.

[10] Satyrs or silens (the two terms are often used synonymously) are depicted in Attic art with the ears, tails, and hooves of horses (or, later on, features of goats); they have receding hairlines, snub noses, and bulging eyes (these are the physical similarities to Socrates); they are usually ithyphallic, lust after wine and sex, and accompany Dionysus.

make with pipes or an aulos in their hands, and when you open them up they are shown to have images of the gods inside. And I say that he is like the satyr Marsyas.[11] Now I don't suppose, Socrates, that you yourself would dispute that you are like them in form. As for how you are like them in other respects too, listen to what's next. You are hubristic.[12] Or aren't you? If you don't agree, I will provide witnesses. Well, aren't you C an aulos player? And a far more amazing one than Marsyas. For he enchants people with an instrument, through the power of his mouth. Even now whoever plays his music on the aulos—for I say that the aulos music of Olympus[13] is that of Marsyas, since Marsyas taught him—his music, whether a good aulos player plays it or some no-good aulos girl, it alone makes the audience possessed, and makes clear which of them have need of the gods and of initiation rites, for it is divine. But you so far surpass him that you do the same thing without an instrument, with D words alone. For whenever we hear other words when someone else is speaking, even a very good speaker, it makes practically no difference to anyone. But whenever anyone hears you, or hears your words from someone else, even if the one who is speaking doesn't amount to much at all, whether a woman hears it or a grown man or a young man, we are all stunned and possessed.

"Now, gentlemen, if I weren't in danger of seeming absolutely drunk, I'd tell you, and swear to it, what his words have done to me and still E do now. Whenever I hear them, my heart leaps far more that those of the corybants,[14] and tears pour from me, thanks to his words, and I see the same thing happening to very many others. When I heard Pericles[15] and other good speakers, I did believe that they were speaking well, but nothing like this happened to me, nor was my soul in an uproar, nor was it upset at how slavish I was. But because of this Marsyas here

---

[11] Marsyas invented, or found, the aulos, which Athena had discarded because it distorted her features. With it he challenged Apollo to a contest in music, Apollo playing the lyre. Marsyas lost and Apollo flayed him alive, turning his skin into a wine jug. For Alcibiades and the aulos see *Alcibiades I*, 106e with note.

[12] Hubris is a gratuitous attack on another's honor: for more on Socratic hubris, see *Alcibiades I*, 114d with note. Satyrs were normally considered hubristic for their sexual assaults; Marsyas may be considered hubristic for daring to compete with Apollo.

[13] The legendary musician Olympus was loved by Marsyas and credited with music which seemed to drive those who heard it out of their minds.

[14] Mythical followers of the nature goddess Cybele, known for their ecstatic drum and aulos music.

[15] On Pericles see *Alcibiades I* 104b and note.

216A many times indeed it seemed to me that life was not worth living for one in my condition.

"And you won't say, Socrates, that this isn't true. Even now I know myself that if I were willing to listen, I'd not be able to tough it out it, but the same thing would happen to me. For he forces me to agree that though I am myself very much wanting I still do not take care of myself but instead manage the affairs of the Athenians. So I force myself to plug my ears and run away from him, as from the Sirens,[16] so I do not end up growing old sitting there at his side.

B "And he's the only person before whom I've experienced something one would think I didn't have in me: being at all ashamed. He is the only one who has ever made me feel ashamed. For I admit that I am unable to argue that it is not necessary do to what he bids me to do. But whenever I leave him, I am overcome by the honor which comes from the many. So I go on the run and flee him, and when I see him, I C am ashamed because of the things I'd agreed with him. There have been many times when I would have been glad to no longer see him among the living, but if this were to happen, I know well that I'd be far more upset. So I just don't know what to do with this man.

"The same thing has happened to many others, thanks to the aulos music coming from this satyr. Listen to something else about how like he is to those I've compared him to and what amazing power he has. D For you can be assured that none of you really knows him. But I will reveal him, since I've begun to. Now you see that Socrates is erotically inclined toward those who are beautiful, and is always around them and is stunned by them and is ignorant about everything and knows nothing. As far as his appearance goes, isn't he like a silen? Very much so. For he's covered outside just like a carved silen. But once he's opened up, my fellow drinkers, how much moderation do you think he's full of? I'd have you know that even if anyone is beautiful, it's no concern E to him at all, but you wouldn't believe how full of contempt he is, nor if someone is wealthy or has any other of all the things that the mob thinks make one happy. He believes that all of these possessions are worth nothing and that we amount to nothing, I'm telling you, and he spends his whole life being ironic[17] and joking with people.

---

[16] The Sirens lure men to them with their enchanting song, and those who are enchanted can never depart (*Odyssey* 12.37-54, 154-200).

[17] Greek *eironeia* more often than not refers to intentional dissembling about one's worth, i.e., mock humility. While Socrates may speak in that way often enough, here and at 218d below his irony seems to be

"I don't know if any one has seen the images within him when he has opened up and was being serious. But I have seen them, and they seemed to me to be so divine and golden and beautiful and wonderful 217A that, in brief, whatever Socrates bid had to be done. Believing that he was serious about my good looks I believed they were a godsend and my wonderful good fortune, thinking that once I'd favored him[18] I would hear everything he knew.

"But it's amazing how much contempt he had for my good looks. With this intention I sent away my servant, though I hadn't been in B the habit of being with him alone, and was alone with him—for I must tell you the whole truth, gentlemen; put your mind to it, and if I say anything that isn't true, Socrates, refute me. As I was saying, I was alone with him, and I thought that he'd say to me the things that a lover says to his beloved when they're alone, and I was glad. But none of this happened, for he talked with me as was his habit, and after spending C the day with me he went off. After this I invited him to exercise with me, and did exercise with him, thinking I'd get somewhere there. Now he did exercise with me and wrestled with me, with no one else there. What's to say? It got me nowhere.

"Since I was making no progress like this, it seemed to me that I was to make an assault on the man at full strength and not to hold back, since I'd taken this in hand, but know once and for all what was going on. I invite him to dinner, no differently than a lover would plot D against his beloved. He didn't agree to this quickly, but in time he was persuaded to come. The first time he came, he wanted to leave after he ate. That time I was ashamed and let him go. But I plotted against him again, and when he had dined I kept talking with him farther and farther into the night, and when he wanted to leave I got him to stay by saying that it was too late. So he took his rest on the couch next to me, on which he had dined, and there was no one else sleeping in the room except for us.

---

something more complex: his habit of saying something that is false in one sense but true in another. Alcibiades understands him better than most.

[18] A euphemism for favors of a sexual sort: Alcibiades is to allow himself to play a passive role in intercourse. Alcibiades assumes, in accordance with the sexual practices of his day, that Socrates, as his lover, would give him something in exchange for intercourse (here, as ought to be the case in the better sort of affair, the something is to be intangible). For Alcibiades, the beloved, is not expected to derive any pleasure from playing the passive role. On Greek sexuality see the note at *Alcibiades I* 103a.

E "Now up to this point what I've said could have been admirably said to anyone. But you wouldn't have heard me saying what follows if it weren't the case that, as the saying goes, 'wine, with or without boys, speaks true,'[19] and that it seems unjust to me to hide Socrates' proud deed once one has embarked on praising him. And what happens to a man who is bitten by a snake happened to me as well. They say that one who has experienced this is unwilling to speak of it except to those 218A who have themselves been bitten, since they alone will understand if he brought himself to do and say anything because of the pain. I was bitten by a more painful thing and in a more painful spot than anyone could be bitten, for I was struck and bitten in the heart, or the soul, or whatever one should call it, by philosophical words, which take fiercer hold of one than a serpent, whenever they get a hold on a soul that is young and not without natural gifts, and make one do or say B anything. As I look around, I see Phaedruses, Agathons, Eryximachuses, Pausaniases, Aristodemuses and Aristophaneses—what need is there to mention Socrates and the rest of you? You've all shared in the madness and frenzy of philosophy, so you will all hear what I've got to say. For you'll understand what was done then and is said now. As for the slaves, and if there's any unholy hick here, shut off your ears with great big doors.

"Now, gentlemen, once the lamp was out and the boys had C left, it seemed to me that I shouldn't try anything fancy, but freely tell him what I thought. So I pushed him and said, 'Socrates, are you sleeping?'

"'Certainly not,' he said.

"'Well, do you know what I've been thinking?'

"'Whatever is it?' he said.

"'I think,' I said, 'that you are the only one worthy of being my lover, and you seem to me to be hesitating to woo me. This is how it is with me: I believe it is completely senseless not to grant you this favor, and D anything else you need of my property or that of my friends. For there is nothing more honorable to me than becoming as good as I can be, and I do not think that when it comes to this there is any more effective helper for me than you. I would be far more ashamed before those who are sensible of not favoring such a man than I would be ashamed of favoring him before the many, who are foolish.'

---

[19] I.e., if one's had enough to drink, one will tell the truth even if the slaves ("boys") are present. Perhaps also an allusion to another saying, "wine and boys are true," i.e., both those who are drunk and children tell the truth.

"And he, when he'd heard this, spoke very ironically and forcefully and very much in keeping with himself: 'My dear friend Alcibiades, you really are probably no nobody, if what you say about me is E true, and there is in me some power to make you better. You'd have spotted an unimaginable beauty in me, you know, and one far superior to the handsome form you have. If looking it over you're attempting to bargain with me and trade beauty for beauty, you intend to get the better of me by far, and are attempting to possess true beauty instead of seeming beauty. You have in mind to really exchange "for gold, 219A bronze."[20] But, you blessed man, consider this better, lest it escape your notice that I don't amount to anything. For, you know, the vision of the mind begins to get sharper when the sight of the eyes begins to fade. And you're far from that point.'

"And I, once I'd heard this, said, 'I've said my bit, and nothing otherwise than as I intend. You yourself give your advice as to what you believe would be best for you and me.'

"'Well,' he said, 'that's well put. For in the time to come we'll advise B one another and do whatever appears best to the two of us concerning this and everything else.'

"Now once I'd heard and said this, and shot my bolt, so to speak, I thought that he was wounded. I got up, did not allow him to say another word, put my mantel around us (it was winter), lay down beneath this C and the little cloak he was using as a blanket, threw my arms around this truly divine and amazing man, and lay there all night long. You won't say, Socrates, that I'm not telling the truth about this. When I'd done this he was so superior to and contemptuous of and mocking of my beauty, and treated it with such hubris—and in this respect, I thought I was really something, gentlemen of the jury, since you are the judges of Socrates' arrogance—be assured, by the gods, by the goddesses, that D when I got up I'd slept the night with Socrates no differently than if I had slept with my father or an older brother.

"After that, what do you think I had in mind? I believed that I had been bested, but admired the nature of this man and his moderation and courage, as I'd encountered a man of a sort I thought I would never encounter when it comes to good sense and endurance. I couldn't bring myself to be angry at him or to be deprived of his company, but I had E no way to win him over. For I knew well that that he was far more

[20] In *Iliad* 6.232–236 the Greek Diomedes traded his bronze armor for the more valuable golden armor of the Trojan ally Glaucus.

invulnerable to money than Ajax was to steel,[21] and the only way I thought he could be captured, he had escaped me. I was at a complete loss, and I wandered about enslaved by this man as no one has ever been enslaved by anyone.

"To add to all of this which had already happened, afterwards we were on the campaign against Potidaea together, and messed together there.[22] First of all, in the labors of the campaign he outdid not only me, but everyone else. Whenever we were cut off somewhere and forced 220A to go without food, as happens in the field, everyone else was nothing when it came to endurance. And he was the only one who was able to enjoy our feasts, particularly whenever he was forced to drink—though he didn't want to; for he outdid everyone and, most amazing of all, nobody has ever seen Socrates drunk. (It seems to me that there will soon be a test of this here.) When it comes to enduring winter—and the B winters are awful there—he did amazing things. One time in particular there was a most awful frost and everyone kept inside or, if they went out, did so covered in an amazing amount of clothing and with their feet wrapped in felt and fleeces. But he would go out in these conditions wearing the same little cloak he was in the habit of wearing before, and unshod he made his way through the ice more easily than those who were shod. The soldiers looked askance at him, thinking he was contemptuous of them.

C "So much for that. But it's worth hearing

What a deed he did and dared, the mighty man[23]

while on campaign there. One day at dawn he was reflecting about something and stood on the spot considering it, and when he did not make progress, he did not go off but stood there continuing to seek it out. It was already noon, and people saw what he was up to, and, amazed, said to each other, 'Socrates has stood since dawn mulling D something over.' Finally some of the Ionians, when it was evening and they'd had their dinner, brought out their bedding, partly to sleep where it was cool (it was summer then), partly to keep watch on him to see if he would stand there through the night. He stood there until dawn broke and the sun came up. Then he went off after making a prayer to the sun.

---

[21] In the *Iliad* Ajax is not completely invulnerable but is very difficult to wound thanks to his massive shield and his skill in battle.

[22] Potidaea, a city in northern Greece, had revolted from Athens in 432, and an Athenian army was sent to reduce the city.

[23] A modified quotation of Homer, *Odyssey* 4.242 or 272: the first, from Menelaus' account of Odysseus' exploits at Troy, the second, from Helen's.

"And if you'd like, in battle—for it is only just to give him credit for this—when the battle took place for which the generals awarded me the E medal for valor, it was no person other than he who saved me. He was unwilling to leave me behind when I was wounded, but saved both my weapons and myself. And then I, Socrates, told the generals to give the medal of valor to you—you won't blame me for this or say that I'm not telling the truth. No, for when the generals looked to my prestige and wanted to give me the medal, you yourself were more eager than the generals that I get it rather than you.

"Now, gentlemen, Socrates was also worth seeing when the army 221A was withdrawing from Delium. I was there in the cavalry, while he was serving on foot. He was withdrawing together with Laches, when our people had already scattered.[24] I met up with him, and as soon as I saw him I told him to take heart and said that I would not leave him behind. I there got a finer look at Socrates than I had at Potideaa (for I was less fearful as I was on horseback). First, I saw how much he B surpassed Laches in keeping his head. Then, Aristophanes, as you've put it, he was "swaggering and throwing his eyes from side to side,"[25] calmly glancing at friends and foes so as to make it clear to all, even from far off, that if anyone attacked this man, he would defend himself very vigorously. Hence both he and his companion got away unhurt. C For in war those who act like this are rarely attacked, but those who flee headlong are pursued.

"Now one could praise Socrates for many other things, and wonderful ones at that. When it comes to everything else about him, someone might say similar things about some other person, but the fact that he is like no other person—neither one of old nor one of the people today—is altogether worthy of wonder. One could liken Achilles to Brasidas and others, or liken Pericles to Nestor and Antenor,[26] as well D as others, and one could liken others in the same way. But this man here is so strange, both he himself and his words, that one couldn't find anyone close, neither among those today nor those of old, unless,

---

[24] In 424 the Athenians were defeated by the Boetians near Delium (in southeastern Boetia) and retreated in a rather disorderly fashion. Laches, an Athenian general (though he was not serving in that capacity at Delium) speaks highly of Socrates' courage at *Laches* 181b.

[25] An adaptation of *Clouds* 362.

[26] Brasidas was the best Spartan general of the first half of the Peloponnesian War; he died in battle in 422. The Greek Nestor and Trojan Antenor were wise counselors during the Trojan War.

that is, one likens him to those I'm talking about, to no man, but to silens and satyrs, both himself and his words.

"Come to think of it, I left this out at the beginning: his words are E also most like to those silens that open up. For if you were willing to listen to Socrates' words, they would seem to be quite laughable at first. That's the sort of phrases and expressions they are wrapped in on the outside, like the hide of a hubristic satyr. For he speaks of pack-donkeys and any old bronzesmiths, cobblers and tanners, and he always seems to be saying the same things in the same way, so any inexperienced and 222A unintelligent person would laugh at his words. But one who sees them opened up and gets inside of them will first find that they are the only words to have any intelligence within them, then that they are most divine and have in them the most images of excellence and the farthest reach—or rather that they touch on everything that one who is to be admirable and good ought to consider.

"This, gentleman, is what I have to say in praise of Socrates. What I have to say in blame of him I mixed in when I said how he treated me B with hubris. Though he didn't do this to me alone, but also to Charmides son of Glaucon and Euthydemus son of Diocles[27] and very many others. He deceives us by acting as if he's in love, but he becomes the one who is loved instead of the one who's in love. I'm telling this to you, Agathon: don't be deceived by him, but learn from what happened to us and be cautious rather than, as the proverb goes, learning your lesson, like the fool, only after it's happened to you."

C When Alcibiades had said this there was much laughter at his frankness, because he still seemed to be in love with Socrates. But Socrates said, "You seem sober to me, Alcibiades. For you wouldn't even have tried to disguise yourself so subtly all around and obscure the reason you said all of this, saying it only at the end, where you put it as a sort of appendage, as if you hadn't said everything for the sake D of driving Agathon and me apart, thinking as you do that I must love you and no other, and Agathon be loved by you and by no other. But you didn't get away with it, as this satyr drama, or silen drama,[28] of

---

[27] Charmides, Plato's uncle, appears as a youth of great beauty and modesty in the dialogue named after him (but went on to be associated with the Thirty Tyrants led by his cousin, Critias). Euthydemus is described as a beauty by Xenophon in *Memorabilia* 4.2, where he plays a role not unlike that Alcibiades himself plays in the Alcibiades dialogues: see introduction, section 3 (he is to be distinguished from the sophist and title character of the *Euthydemus*).

[28] A satyr drama regularly followed the three tragedies put on at the City Dionysia; such plays were comical, and usually featured a chorus of satyrs.

yours was quite clear. Just, Agathon, don't let it do him any good, but prepare yourself so that no one drives us apart."

Now Agathon said, "Indeed, Socrates, what you say is probably E true. I reckon that this is why he lay down between me and you, to separate us. It will do him no good: I'm coming over to lie down by you."

"Zeus!" said Alcibiades, "look at what this man is doing to me! He thinks that he must outdo me everywhere. At least, you amazing man, let Agathon lie down in between us."

"But that's not possible," said Socrates. "For you've praised me, and I must praise the person on my right. So if Agathon lies down below you, surely he'll praise me instead of being praised by me, won't he?[29] 223A Just leave it be, you wild man, and don't resent the lad being praised by me. For I do really desire to sing his praises."

"Alas and alack," said Agathon, "Alcibiades, there's no way I'm going to remain here, for it is dead certain that I will change places so I can be praised by Socrates."

"This," said Alcibiades, "is just what always happens. When Socrates is around it's impossible for anyone else to share the beautiful ones. How easily he's found a persuasive argument even now to get this man to lie at his side."

B So Agathon stood up to sit by Socrates' side. But suddenly a great many people partying came to the door; they found it open, as someone had gone out, and came straight in and lay down beside them. Everything was full of confusion, and as there was no longer any order they were forced to drink a great deal of wine. . . .

The dialogue ends a page later with Aristodemus' vague recollection of Socrates getting Aristophanes and Agathon to agree, after the other guests had left, that the same man would know how to compose both comedy and tragedy. Socrates then goes off at dawn, after drinking all night, and spends his day as usual.

[29] Compare 214c.

AESCHINES OF SPHETTUS, *ALCIBIADES*

The text for this translation and the numbering of the fragments are taken from Socratis et Socraticorum Reliquiae, *ed. Gabriele Giannantoni (Naples 1990). Words taken to be Aeschines' own are printed in* Roman ten-point type; *those given for context appear in* sans serif nine-point type.

1. Maximus of Tyre, *Lectures* VII ("Which diseases are more difficult, those of the body or those of the soul?") 7.[1]

Alcibiades is sick; a great, wild fire feeds on him, throws his thoughts into a confusion most like madness, and carries him about everywhere: from the Lyceum to the Assembly, from the Assembly to the sea, from the sea to Sicily . . .

Maximus of Tyre, *Lectures* VI ("What is knowledge?") 6.

It is in breaking this [divine] law that Alcibiades met with ill fortune, not when the Athenians recalled him from Sicily, nor when

him the Heralds and Eumolpidae did curse

nor when he fled in exile from Attica. These are small things, and a condemnation easily despised; for this man was superior even in exile to those remaining at home (for he found favor in exile among the Spartans, he fortified Decelea, he was an ally of Tissaphernes, and he led the Peloponnesians). But the true judgment against Alcibiades was more important by far, based on a more important law and given by more important judges. It was when he left the Lyceum, and was condemned by Socrates, and banished by philosophy that he fled in exile, then that he was convicted. O bitter condemnation, implacable curse, pitiful wanderings! Therefore the Athenians, having even entreated for his return, took him back, but philosophy and knowledge and excellence remain

---

[1] The two passages from the second century A.D. philosophizing orator Maximus of Tyre are included largely because they show that the second fragment is indeed a reference to our dialogue. They thus confirm that Socrates' conversation with Alcibiades took place in the Lyceum, the gymnasium just outside of Athens, which was a frequent haunt of Socrates and would later house Aristotle's school.

unapproachable and irreconcilable once one has fled from them. Such a thing is knowledge, and such a thing ignorance.

2. [Demetrius], *On Style* 205.[2]

Often we employ trimeters[3] as phrases and sometimes as clauses, as when Plato says, "I went down yesterday to the Piraeus with Glaucon" [the first words of the *Republic*]; for the pauses and cadences are frequent. And Aeschines says:

We were sitting on the seats in the Lyceum, where the officials set up the playing field.

3. Priscian, *Institutes of Grammar* XVIII 297.[4]

Aeschines in the *Alcibiades*:

But he,[5] who had as easily as anyone reached fifty . . .

4. Athenaeus, *The Learned Banquet* XIV 656F.[6]

Aeschines uses *dephakia* ("little pigs") thus in the *Alcibiades*:

Just as the huckster women raise their little pigs . . .

5. Aelius Aristides, *In Defense of the Four*, 575.[7]

Plato's speeches [in the *Alcibiades I*] were directed against a man who not

---

[2] The treatise *On Style* is traditionally attributed to Demetrius of Phaleron, the Peripatetic philosopher and ruler of Athens under Macedon in the later fourth century B.C.; but the treatise was apparently composed much later, by an unknown author.

[3] Prose trimeters, less strictly measured than those of verse.

[4] Priscian was a Latin grammarian active around 500 A.D.; Priscian used Greek examples to help his mainly Greek-speaking readers learn the niceties of Latin.

[5] Perhaps Themistocles, who was ostracized in the later 470s when he would have been around fifty. At *Alcibiades I* 127e, Socrates makes fifty the age by which one should have already cared for oneself; this is perhaps more than coincidence.

[6] Athenaeus, who was active around A.D. 200, gathered together excerpts from earlier authors, many from texts no longer extant, under the guise of a learned conversation at a lengthy dinner party.

[7] The second century A.D. Greek orator Aelius Aristides quotes Aeschines in two speeches attacking Plato, *On Oratory* (fragment 12 below) and *In Defense of the Four* (fragments 5, 8, 9, 10). The four are the four statesmen Plato attacks in the *Gorgias* (503c, 515d): Miltiades, Themistocles, Pericles, and Cimon. Here Aristides' point is that Plato should not have slandered Pericles to Alcibiades, of all people. In fragment 9 below, the continuation of this passage, Aristides lauds Aeschines for having Socrates praise Themistocles to Alcibiades.

only readily despised Pericles but, as Aeschines says about him, was the sort who

would have most gladly rebuked the twelve gods.[8]

So great was his excess of pride and of thinking no one worthy of anything.

6. Cicero, *Tusculan Disputations* III 32, 77.

For what are we to say, since Socrates persuaded Alcibiades, as we hear, that he was no man at all, and that there was not a bit of difference between Alcibiades, though of the highest birth, and some porter?

Augustine, *City of God* XIV 8.

For they say that Alcibiades also (if the man's name does not escape me), although he seemed to himself to be blessed, upon Socrates disagreeing and showing that he was wretched because he was stupid, wept. For him, therefore, stupidity was the cause of that misery that is useful and desirable, through which a man mourns that he is what he ought not to be. The Stoics, however, say that it is not the stupid man but the wise man who cannot be miserable.

7. Oxyrhynchus Papyrus 1608, column I, fragment 1.[9]

". . . concerning your own parents to have been as Themistocles[10] is said to have been concerning his?"

"Hush, Socrates," he said.

"Does it seem to you that it is necessary that men be unskilled in music before becoming skilled in it? And unskilled regarding horses before becoming skilled regarding them?"

---

[8] The twelve gods, usually identified with the Olympians, are those of the altar in the Athenian Agora that was the heart of Athens, a place where suppliants sought sanctuary and the point from which Athenians measured distances.

[9] The papyrus, one of many found at the Egyptian town of Oxyrhynchus, dates to the later part of the second century A.D. Other fragments of the papyrus, not quoted here, are largely unintelligible, but do identify the work since they match fragments 8 and 9 below, and also confirm that fragment 9 below follows immediately upon fragment 8.

[10] Themistocles (c. 524–459 B.C.) was Athens' leading general during the battles against the Persians of 480. At Salamis he played the crucial role in keeping the Greek allies from retreating and tricked the Persians into attacking in the narrow strait where their superior numbers were of little effect. Sometime during the later 470s he was ostracized by the Athenians, and was subsequently hounded from Greece and then condemned to death by the Athenians on the charge of sympathizing with the Persians. He was also thought to have extorted money from fellow Greeks (Herodotus 8.111–112).

"It seems to me necessary to be unskilled in music or unskilled in horses first."

"Then . . .

(fragment 4 of the same papyrus)

. . . and Apollodorus[11] to give a fine defense of the base one.

"But as to that," he [Alcibiades] said, "I could not believe that Themistocles was disinherited by his father. Aren't such things the mark of a base man and don't they amount to great folly—when anyone comes into such great disagreement and into the greatest hostility with his own parents? Even a child would find a way of avoiding this."

"Do you believe that it is such a small matter, Alcibiades," I said, "to be cast out by one's parents, so that just any man . . . "

8. Aelius Aristides, *In Defense of the Four* 575.

Therefore his [Aeschines'] Socrates does not follow the same path, but says what?

I, recognizing that he was envious of Themistocles . . . .

Then comes the praise of Themistocles, fitting on two accounts, I think, since it is true and since the speech was timely for the youth.

9. Aelius Aristides, *In Defense of the Four* 348-349.

Let us consider what sort of things Aeschines, the companion of Socrates and fellow pilgrim of Plato, tells us about Themistocles.

[I, recognizing that he was envious of Themistocles, said,] "Since you have brought yourself to attack the life of Themistocles, consider what sort of man you thought it fitting to condemn. Think about where the sun rises and where it sets."

"But it is nothing hard to know such things, Socrates," he said.

"Have you ever given any thought to the fact that the land called Asia, a land as large as that the sun crosses, is ruled by a single man?"

"Of course," he said, "the Great King."

"You know, then, that that man led an army here and against the Lacedaemonians, believing that if he conquered this pair of cities the rest of the Greeks would readily be subservient to him. And he struck such fear into the Athenians that they abandoned their land and fled to Salamis, and, choosing Themistocles as their general, they turned it over to him to do whatever he wished with their affairs. And their greatest hope of salvation lay in whatever advice he gave on their behalf. And in

[11] Apollodorus' role in this fragment and the dialogue, and even his identity, are uncertain.

that situation Themistocles was not disheartened because in number of ships and infantry and money the resources of the Greeks were lacking and those of the king were superior, but he knew that unless that man excelled him in giving advice all these other things, great as they were in magnitude, would not be of any great help to him. This, too, he knew, that whichever people had men more worthy in excellence overseeing their affairs, it was their side that was usually victorious. And then at last the king sensed that his side was the weaker, on that day when he encountered a man more worthy than himself.

"And Themistocles so easily handled the great resources of this man that after he had beaten him in a sea battle he wanted to persuade the Athenians to destroy the bridge[12] that the king had built. But when he was not able to do this, he sent a message to the king telling him the opposite of what had been decided by the city, that when the Athenians told him to destroy the bridge he himself had opposed them, trying to save the king and those with him. The result was that not only we and the rest of the Greeks believed that Themistocles was the cause of our salvation, but even the king who had been defeated by Themistocles believed that he had been saved by that man alone. To such a great extent Themistocles surpassed him in intelligence.

"Therefore when he became an exile from his city the king gave thanks to him on the ground that Themistocles had saved him, and gave him many gifts and also rule over all of Magnesia,[13] so that even when he was in exile Themistocles' affairs were in a better state than those of many Athenians who were thought to be good and admirable and remained at home. At that time, then, who could justly lay claim to having the greatest power, other than Themistocles, who as general of the Greeks defeated the king who ruled those from the sun's rising to its setting?

"Consider then," I said, "Alcibiades, that even for such a man as he was, his knowledge, great as it was, was not enough to protect him from being banished and disenfranchised by his city, but was wanting. What do you think will happen to lesser men who do not take care of themselves? Is it not surprising if they are able to do even the least things right?

"And do not," I said, "Alcibiades, charge me with being unusual or irreligious when it comes to fortune and divine affairs, if I attribute to that man knowledge of all that he did and believe that fortune was not responsible for these deeds. For I could far more show you that those

---

[12] The bridge was that across the Hellespont, which allowed the Persian army to cross back to Asia.

[13] The city of Magnesia on the Meander, in central Asia Minor.

who hold the opposite view to mine are irreligious than they could show me to be, they who believe that fortune comes equally to bad and good men, and that good and admirable men, at least if they are more pious, do not receive better things from the gods."

Surely the Socrates speaking here [i.e., Aeschines' Socrates] is the same as the one speaking earlier [Plato's Socrates].

10. Aelius Aristides, *In Defense of the Four* 576-577.

And he [Socrates] does not speak ill of Themistocles in his [Alcibiades'] presence, in order that he not be corrupted further in hearing this, nor is Alcibiades excused on the grounds that it is not he alone that lives in ignorance, but all those who handle the affairs of the city. Not at all, for he forces him

to cry out, disheartened, placing his head on his knees, since he was not even close to Themistocles in preparation.

And in addition he fittingly strengthens the speech. For in the middle of it he says that not even such great knowledge sufficed for him, but fell short; he does this so that the slander is removed, while what is useful in exhortation is kept, both in the praise, and in saying that not even these things sufficed for Themistocles. In this way although Aeschines falls short of Plato in other areas, he handles this somehow better.

Plutarch, *How To Distinguish a Flatterer from a Friend* 29, 69e-f.

In what situations, then, should a friend be forceful, and when should he use intense honesty? Whenever circumstances bid him to lay into raging pleasure, or anger, or hubris, or chastise greed, or check senseless insensitivity . . . . Thus Socrates chastised Alcibiades, and produced a truthful tear from him as he was refuted, and turned his heart.

11. Cicero, *Tusculan Disputations* III 32, 77-78 (continuation of Cicero's text from fragment 6).

When Alcibiades was downcast, and, crying, begged Socrates to give him excellence and drive away his baseness, what are we to say, Cleanthes? That there was nothing bad in this thing, which made Alcibiades feel wretched? . . . What then? Didn't Alcibiades' sickness consist of the evils and vices of his soul?

12. Aelius Aristides, *In Defense of Oratory* 61-64.[14]

Come, then, and I will provide "from the same school," in the words of Plato, another witness, not just a likeness. For Plato will not be upset if Aeschines votes in agreement with what Plato has said:

---

[14] Aristides refers to *Gorgias* 493d, where Plato has Socrates introduce another likeness "from the same school," there the example of the water carriers. In his defense of rhetoric, Aristides has granted, for the sake of argument, that rhetoric is not an art, and has been making use of passages from the *Phaedrus* to show that inspiration, as well as art, can be of value.

If I believed that I was able to be beneficial through some art, I would convict myself of great idiocy. But as it is I believed that this had been granted me by a divine dispensation in Alcibiades' case. And none of this is worthy of wonder.

You are listening to a man who is your comrade and who believes the same man was wisest that you do, and I add that he attributes his words to the same man you attribute words to. "One must not," he [Aeschines] says, "wonder, Plato, if even someone who does not possess an art is able to benefit mankind."

For many sick men become well, some by human art, some by divine dispensation. Now those who became well through human art are treated by doctors, but those who became well through divine dispensation are led by desire to what will be useful: they desired to vomit, whenever this would be advantageous, and to go hunting, whenever exercise would be advantageous.

Heracles! How explicitly and clearly Aeschines, the fellow pilgrim of Plato, attests to Plato that the arguments of his that we brought forward a little while ago are more in accord with human nature and more admirable in the eyes of the gods than the other arguments he contrived for the sake of paradox. And Aeschines is clearly testifying to us just like a man summoned by a herald, and he seals, as it were, Plato's testimony; for he confirms the words of Plato that support our case.

Aelius Aristides, *In Defense of Oratory* 74

Therefore although I was citing testimony I was forced to testify myself in favor of the argument. But I will return to the remainder of the testimony:

And I, through the love that I had for Alcibiades, felt just as the Bacchants do. For whenever they are inspired they draw honey and milk where others cannot even draw water. And I, though knowing no lesson through which I could benefit a man by teaching, nevertheless believed that by being together with this man I could make him better through love.

Thus he ends on this point of conversation, not with riddles, nor with a hidden meaning, nor only in some way saying the same things we do, but as if he composed them on purpose to be of use to us.

13. Plutarch, *Life of Alcibiades* 4.1-4 (193 a-c).[15]

Already many of noble birth thronged him [Alcibiades] and followed him about. The others clearly were stricken by the brilliance of his youthful beauty and paid court to it, but Socrates' love was great testimony to the youth's excellence and good nature, which he saw manifested in his appearance and shining through.

---

[15] This passage is based on a variety of sources in addition to Aeschines, but it is well worth including here as a specimen of the riches of Plutarch's *Life of Alcibiades*. The most likely reference to Aeschines' work is Plutarch's statement near the end of this passage that Alcibiades recognized Socrates' service to the gods in his care for the youth and their salvation.

But he feared his wealth and prestige and the mob of citizens, foreigners, and allies who tried to win him over with flattery and favors. This he was able to ward off, and not see him, like a plant in bloom, lose and corrupt its proper fruit. For fortune has never so taken hold of anyone from without and enclosed him with so-called goods so as to make him invulnerable to philosophy and unapproachable by words having any honesty or bite in them.

Soon, when he made himself a companion of Socrates and had heard the words not of a suitor hunting unmanly pleasure or begging for kisses and caresses, but refuting what was unsound in his soul and driving out his empty and senseless vanity,

he cowered like a defeated cock lowering its wing.[16]

And he believed that Socrates' undertaking was in reality service of the gods for the sake of care of the youth and their salvation. And thinking little of himself, full of wonder at Socrates, delighting in philosophy, and ashamed before excellence, without noticing it he came to possess the "image of love, reciprocal love," as Plato calls it,[17] with the result that all were full of wonder at seeing him dining with Socrates and wrestling with him and tenting with him, while he was difficult with his other suitors and hard to win over, and to some behaved quite arrogantly, as with Anytus son of Anthemion.[18]

---

[16] The line is attributed (as fragment 17) to the comic poet Phrynichus, a contemporary of Aristophanes.

[17] *Phaedrus* 255d.

[18] Plutarch goes on to relate that Alcibiades, after rejecting a dinner invitation from Anytus, crashed the same party and had his slaves steal half of Anytus' best silver. When Anytus' other guests complained of Alcibiades' hubris, Anytus was still smitten enough to reply that Alcibiades had acted kindly by taking only half. Anytus son of Anthemion appears also in the *Meno* (89e-95a), and would be one of Socrates' accusers (*Apology* 23e).